Miracle Escape

from the Clutches of Stalin

A Memoir of Life in Eastern Poland under
Soviet Occupation, 1939-1941

Larisa Moshar

Miracle Escape

from the Clutches of Stalin

The Changing River of Life
Heraclitus, 540-475 BC

PUBLISHED BY
Market House Book Co
PO Box 17222
Seattle, Washington 98107

Library of Congress Cataloging-in-Publication Data: 2005920017

Moshar, Larisa
Miracle Escape

ISBN 0-944638-64-3 $19.95
Printed and bound in the United States of America.
1 2 3 4 5 6 7 8 9

Cover Design: Ashley Knecht
Art Work: Lin Wang

Acknowledgments

For some reason unknown to me I want to use the name of my ancestor great, great, great... great grandfather Moshar. In the fourteenth century Russia was overrun by hoards of Tartars. Russia remained under their yoke for 300 years. I was told there was a Prince Moshar who married a Russian girl named Anastasia. Over the years, the name was Russianized and became Mosharovsky. That was my mother's maiden name. Her first name was also Anastasia.

I want to give my sincere thanks to my good friend Val Dmitrief, who encouraged me to write this book and helped me with writing it.

This book is a true account detailing my personal experiences in Poland, during two years under a Communist regime. Now I turn my attention to the next book, which will account for two years under a German regime and how I came to America.

Larisa, Seattle 2006

Contents

I want to dedicate *Miracle Escape* to my children: George, Elaine, Richard and Anita. I hope it will help them and other young adults to understand how fortunate they are to be Americans. To be free and to know the feeling of that precious word *freedom*. To appreciate life in this wonderful country and if necessary to fight for that freedom.

Larisa, Seattle 2006.

1 Pre~war Life

M y parents were having their weekly bridge party. I watched the game for a while, but in spite of open windows, it was too hot in the house, so I went outside onto the balcony and stretched out on one of the chaise lounges.

"What a beautiful night," I whispered, filling my lungs with the evening's fresh air, which carried a wonderful smell of flowers and ripening fruits.

August in 1939, in the Southern part of Poland, was especially hot. It was hard to imagine that school would start in a week. I closed my eyes and let my thoughts wander. Yes, that was a very interesting summer for me. In July, my parents and I went to Warsaw, boarded a ship on the river Vistula and went up to Danzig. We stayed two weeks at the Jastarnia Sea resort.

We were supposed to stay one more week in Gdynia, another port on the Baltic Sea, but father decided to cut his vacation short, as the world situation had become very serious. I was well versed in politics because I listened to adult conversations that centered on nothing but the dangers facing us. I Learned that Hitler had already invaded the Rhineland, the Saar, and Austria. My father said Hitler's advances were very threatening, especially when he took over Czechoslovakia. I was worried when I heard that it was possible that Poland would be the next target. It appeared that the geographical location of Poland was not to her advantage. Situated between two powers, Germany and Russia, it had been partitioned three times in history.

After World War I and the Treaty of Versailles, Poland finally won her independence — a free and democratic country at last. Was her freedom to be threatened again? The German propaganda machine was carrying on a violent campaign against the Poles. Things were unsettled when, in the middle of August 1939, we returned home from our vacation.

The city was nervous, the inevitability of war was almost certain, not only in Poland, but in the whole of Western Europe. There was a partial mobilization of armed forces in Poland.

Why were there to be more wars? I thought. *Had not my parents gone through enough during the First World War and the Russian Revolution?* And how lucky they were to have escaped to Poland and built themselves a good and prosperous life. I thought about my parents. They were both born in Russia before the turn of the century. They met in St. Petersburg, now Leningrad, where they both attended the University. They were married after father's graduation from law school, May 1916, the second year of the war with Germany. Being very patriotic, father enlisted in the St. Michael School of Artillery, and after six months of accelerated training, he was sent, as a Second Lieutenant, to the front lines.

Father had been fighting Germans for two years when the communist revolution swept like a hurricane over Russia. These were horrible times. Luckily, mother and father and my older sister, Nina, fled to Poland. My father was the only one from his family who left Russia. His parents, his older brother, and his brother's wife perished during the revolution. Mother's two brothers and father also fled to Poland but did not stay long and proceeded to Dresden. Her third brother could not escape and was sent to a Siberian concentration camp. Her brother's wife committed suicide under the wheels of a train. Their sixteen-year-old son found his father's pistol and shot himself. Thousands of Russians fled to the free countries all over the world, but millions perished under communist rule in the homeland.

At first, life was not easy for my parents, although they both knew the Polish language (some of their ancestors were Polish), which was a significant advantage for them. For a few years, mother was employed as a grade school teacher until father established himself as a lawyer.

In the spring, the river would overflow and surround the castle

When I was born, things were going quite well for my family. In a few years, a house was built on a hill overlooking an old Lubart Castle dating from the 13ᵗʰ century. A mile away was a swift and clean river. In the spring, it would overflow and surround the castle, which looked majestic and mysterious in the moonlight.

Our house stood on an acre of land. There were fruit trees, shrubs and lots of flowers. Two flights of stairs led to a balcony and the entrance. We had one servant living in the house. A man came to attend to the grounds and do odd jobs.

Within a short time, father built a small house next to ours for mother's friend, Aunt Maria. She was divorced, and had a boy named Vasia.

Vasia was three years older than I, and we grew up together. He was like an older brother to me, and we fought like brother and sister, especially during the preceding summer. He was raising big spiders, the kind that spread their big thick cobwebs in the bushes. He would threaten to turn a spider on me if I didn't steal cigarettes from father (father had all kinds of cigarettes and cigars for his guests. He never smoked). Oh, how I hated Vasia, but that was last summer. This year he was being so nice to me that it got on my nerves. Ha, the secret was that Vasia liked my best friend, Tonia, but she could not have cared less for him. No way was I going to help him, remembering the spider terror.

Suddenly my thoughts were interrupted by loud voices coming through the open windows in the living room. The bridge party was over, and of course father and the judge—his best friend—were already bickering. *What are they talking about?* I listened for a while. *Oh, yes, about yesterday's big announcement.* Yesterday, August twenty-third, the Soviet Union and Nazi Germany Pact was signed. It was an agreement of non-aggression and neutrality between those two countries.

"Don't you understand, Vladimir (my father's name) that treaty poses an enormous threat to Poland and the rest of Europe?" The judge's voice was thundering. "I'm sure there will be a fourth partitioning of Poland. You can't trust these super villains, Hitler and Stalin."

"Wait, Judge," father's voice was mild. "Don't get too nervous, you're forgetting France and England. France and England, maybe even the United States, promised to assist us if Hitler tries to invade Poland."

"So they will. I believe they might start a war with Germany, but what good will it do if the Red Army crosses the border? Stalin's hordes could be in our city overnight. What will happen to you then, my dear friend?" I could almost see the judge's face grinning sarcastically.

"In Stalin's eyes you are a runaway slave, so—"

"All right," father interrupted, "and do you think communists will pat *you* on the head?"

"Gentlemen, gentlemen, please stop," mother's voice was pleading. "Let's not talk about such terrible things."

I did not want to listen any more, either. Anyway, it was time to go to bed. Tonight it was hard to fall asleep. The talk about war was so scary. *Was my smooth and peaceful life threatened?*

It was a good life with a warm and happy family, mother and father, my sister Nina, and I. Nina was married in February of this year and went to live with her husband in another part of Poland—close to the German border. For the last four years she attended the University of Warsaw, coming home for the holidays and summer vacation. I could hardly wait to hear the fascinating stories about her life in the capitol, her studies, fancy balls and dances. This summer I missed her very much. I was fourteen years old and almost five feet and eight inches tall. Since the last summer I had grown several inches which pleased me enormously. I felt almost grown up. My two long braids of reddish blond hair, which were always dangling on both sides of my head, I now wore in a Grecian style bound upon the back of my head. I thought it made me look older and more sophisticated.

Two more years of high school and I would go to Warsaw and enter the Conservatory of Music. I wished to become a pianist. I practiced very hard since the age of five, and my teachers predicted a good future for me. I dreamed of living in big cities and traveling all over the world. The future looked promising and exciting, but now the judge thought we would be invaded by the Soviets. It must have been very late when I finally fell asleep. I tossed and turned for hours.

A noise woke me up. I listened for a while and it sounded as if rocks were bouncing off my window. *What is going on?* I jumped out of bed, put on my robe and opened the shutters. Vasia was sitting on the bench in the garden.

"What do you think you are doing, throwing rocks? You want to break the window? You woke me up!"

"It's about time. First of all, these are not rocks, but pieces of dry dirt. Second, it is after nine o'clock." He grinned at me.

"So what's it to you?" I demanded.

"Look, it is a beautiful day. We won't have many more like this, so I thought we might go to the river gorge for the day."

Now I knew what was on Vasia's mind.

"Just you and me?" I asked innocently.

"Well," he seemed to be embarrassed. "You, I and Tonia."

"And Tonia, of course." I teased. "Lost your heart, huh?"

"Stop it, Lara." Vasia sounded angry. "Don't rub it in. There are still spiders out there in the bushes."

"Don't you dare." Now I was getting annoyed.

Vasia rose from the bench. "All right, all right, you girls don't want my company. Fine." He started moving toward his house.

"Wait, you silly boy." I laughed. "Let's stop fighting. Give me half an hour and we can go to Tonia's together."

Vasia's face brightened.

I started dressing. Funny Vasia, I thought, he was never interested in girls, always making fun of them, and now this infatuation with Tonia. Vasia was eighteen years old, of medium height, with slightly curly brown hair, brown eyes, and a happy-go-lucky disposition. He was fun to be with. In June he graduated from high school and, to the dismay of his mother, did not apply to the University but was looking for a job. In spite of all our bickering, I had a soft spot in my heart for him. With a slight knock, mother came into my room.

"Sleep well, Lara?" She smiled at me.

"Yes, but not enough. I fell asleep late, and now Vasia woke me up."

"But it's almost 10 o'clock."

"I know, I know," I said, packing a bathing suit and towel.

"Going swimming?"

"Yes. Vasia wants us, that is me and Tonia, to go to the river. We'll probably get kayaks at the club, and go up the river and then float down. If that's all right with you, mama?" I asked pleadingly.

"Of course you may go, providing your bed is made and the room cleaned. Look, Lara, your clothes are everywhere—books and magazines on the floor."

I felt uncomfortable. "But, mama, Lida will clean it." Lida had been our servant for years. "She usually does."

Mother frowned, her voice sharpened. "Lida has enough to do. Oh, my God, you always get away with so many things. Yesterday I heard you ask Lida to bring you a glass of water. Couldn't you get it yourself?"

"But, mama..."

"No buts. This has to end, my dear daughter. I should be more strict with you. Besides cleaning your room, you ought to help in the kitchen as well. I am sure you don't even know how to cook eggs."

I came close to mother and gave her a big hug. This approach always worked. "Mama dearest, when school starts, I promise... No, I really promise, I will be a model girl. I even promise to scrub floors."

"Nobody is asking you to scrub floors, just keep your room clean." Mama's voice was already softer.

Through the window I saw Vasia making faces at me and pointing to his wrist. My mother saw him, too.

"Oh, all right, go, only because it is so nice out now, but you have to eat breakfast."

I gave her a kiss. "Yes, yes, I will, and thank you, dearest." I stopped at the doorway and added, "It is very simple to cook eggs. You put them in boiling water and boil them until they are soft."

Mother shook her head, but smiled.

The rest of the week passed quickly.

2   INVASION

On Sunday, September 1st, I woke early in the morning and went outside to pick a couple of apples from the tree. The day promised to be good with the sun shining from a cloudless sky. Biting the apple, I switched on the radio. Instead of the usual music, I heard the nervous voice of a commentator making a strange announcement. Something unusual was happening. Listening for a while, I understood The German army, without any declaration of war, had crossed the Polish border. The Luftwaffe was bombing the nearby cities. War had started.

In the following days the news was depressing and shattering. The Polish army, badly deployed, only partially mobilized and desperately short of modern equipment was no match for the German military machine. Still, Poland was the first country to resist Nazi aggression. The British and French declaration of war on September third was, for the time being, only a gesture.

Within a week Hitler's forces had occupied the western part of Poland and were closing in on Warsaw. Despite the customary heroism of Polish soldiers, the army was in full retreat. By the middle of September, Warsaw was encircled and the campaign reached its final stage.

Our city, Lutsk, being in the eastern part of Poland, was still far from the front lines. It was the capital in the state of Wolhynien, a little over 100 kilometers from the Soviet border, with a population of 45,000, a mixture of Polish, Ukrainian, Russian and Jewish residents. Soon refugees started to pour in from the west. With each day the news became more and more grim. The Germans advanced steadily, bombarding their way eastward as they approached our town.

As father worried about the increasing threat of air raids, our friends, a retired couple, invited us to move to their small country estate on the outskirts of town. Father accepted their offer, and the next day we left Lutsk.

The estate was beautifully picturesque. It consisted of a spacious old house with a large front porch, a winding stream in the meadows, and an orchard full of apple, pear and plum trees. There were many mushrooms, which I loved to pick in the nearby woods. Leaves were starting to turn yellow and red, shimmering like old gold in the warm sun. The beauty of autumn was in full spectrum. I loved the place.

A few days passed quietly. Here the war seemed unreal and was brought to mind only by radio broadcasts. The Warsaw radio station was already silenced by the German invaders, and so we could listen only to a station in Lvov, a big city not far from the Soviet Union border.

On September 17th we were drinking tea with freshly baked pastries. It was a lovely afternoon. Conversation lingered on yesterday's and this morning's news. It seemed strange that since the day before yesterday, the Germans had stopped advancing.

"I wonder what is going on," father said and turning towards me, added, "Lara, dear, will you go and listen to the news and let us know if there are any new developments?"

I went into the house and turned on the radio. Strange! The broadcast was in Russian.

Why in Russian? Maybe I have the wrong station, I thought. But the only radio station we had was in Lvov. I continued to listen.

After a while I understood. Early this morning the Soviet Red Army crossed the Polish border. Soviet forces already occupied Lvov.

"Oh, God," I murmured, "The Soviets are coming here!"

Choked with fear, I ran out of the house shouting.

"Mama, papa, the Red Army crossed the border. Lvov is taken!"

Father jumped from his chair. "What are you saying, child?" He came close to me, grabbed my shoulders and shook me. "This is no time for nonsense, Lara." Papa's voice was angry.

"The radio, papa, the radio! I just heard it."

He let go of me. We all rushed inside and gathered around the receiver.

The voice of the commentator sounded loud and clear: "A victorious Red Army is stretching a helping hand to the people of Poland, liberating them from capitalistic oppression."

The facts were clear. We were as of now under Soviet rule.

Horror stricken, we stood in silence. Father's face was white as chalk. Then mama said in a trembling voice, "Dima, you have to run. Go west. Leave right now while there's time."

Father looked at her not willing to understand. "What are you saying, Nana?"

"I'm saying that you must flee. If you stay, the communists will kill you like they killed your family during the revolution."

Father shook his head. "Where can I go on foot? I've only a little money with me."

"Here," mama said, taking off a big diamond ring, then another with a sapphire, and a heavy gold chain. "Here, these might help."

"I can give you a buggy and a horse," our host added.

Father did not answer. His eyes were fixed on something far away. Silence enveloped us. Finally he whispered. "I can't run and leave my wife and daughter behind. Whatever comes, we're all in this together, and God help us."

There was no use arguing with him, and there was no point in remaining with our friends. We packed our things and returned to our home in town.

The next morning the first tanks of the Red army entered our city. There was no resistance. This aggression was completely unexpected. In confusion, there were rumors that the Soviets came to fight against the Germans, but soon we learned that the August Soviet-Nazi pact was in reality a secret protocol, which partitioned Poland and much of Eastern Europe. The Germans allotted Lithuania, Estonia, Latvia (the Baltic states), and also Bessarabia to the Soviets. Now the German menace was surpassed a thousand times by the unexpected horrors of communist advances. For three days, tanks and army equipment rolled westward. I remembered the judge's words of a week ago, "…a fourth partition of Poland." Father went into town several times, returning home more depressed with each excursion.

"I tried to talk to some soldiers," he said, "and they are so different from the Russian soldiers I knew during the First World War, even the language is somehow changed. Well, old Russia doesn't exist any more. They're a new breed; these Soviet people." As a former officer of the Russian Imperial Army, and most of all, as an escapee from the Soviet Union, father had a great deal to fear from Stalin.

What is going to happen to us now? I wondered. The house seemed suddenly so big and empty with just the three of us. The servants had left.

One day my friend Tonia and I went to town. The streets were jammed with huge tanks, trucks, and other army equipment. Soldiers looked at us suspiciously, and we viewed them with fear. They were mostly young men, about twenty years old, and poorly dressed. Their faces looked pallid and many of them were covered with pox marks.

After the Red Army passed through, the NKVD moved into the sturdiest building in town. The NKVD were Stalin's Secret Police, the fiercest police force in the world. The civilian officials who followed were placed in all the top administrative positions.

On September twenty-eight, the terms of the Soviet-German agreement were published. Poland was now divided almost in half between the two powers. Everybody had to register and were given Soviet passports, thus automatically they became Soviet citizens whether they wanted to or not.

Freedom of movement was restricted. Without permission of the authorities, one could not change a place of dwelling, even to visit another town— special authorization was necessary.

Radio announcements were full of communistic propaganda. We had to hear constantly how happy the population was to be "liberated" from capitalistic oppression and exploitation. A joke began to circulate that yes, we were liberated, but liberated from the good life we had. The communist party and Stalin were praised and glorified. His portrait and that of his comrades appeared everywhere.

From books and what my parents had told me, I knew that there probably never had been a more cruel ruler in history, nor one whose power was so absolute as Stalin's. After the revolution, he rose to power through extraordinary organizational skills, the ability to manipulate people, and absolute ruthlessness. By eliminating everybody standing in his way, he achieved the supreme position and in order to keep it, ruled with bloody terror. Millions of people who, in Stalin's sick mind, could be a threat to him, perished under a firing squad or in remote concentration camps. Terror was so great that survival was possible only with total submission and constant manifestation of gratitude, praise and adoration of Stalin. Poems, songs, and novels presented him as the embodiment of wisdom. Cities, towns, factories, institutions, even mountains in the U.S.S.R. were named after him. Every newspaper and book exalted him as a summit of all that was true, noble and wise. The populace had to agree, applaud and accept unanimously the will of a man who scarcely left a family on Russian land untouched by tragedy.

For twenty years the people of Russia had suffered under Stalin's oppression, and now it was beginning to spill into the helpless states of the West. In our town the NKVD already mobilized spies and informers.

Anything mentioned against the new order had to be reported to the authorities. Criticism, even slight, was absolutely impossible and if any occurred, was punished by instant imprisonment.

The result was that everyone was afraid of everybody else.

3   CHANGES

Soon the process of switching to the Soviet economy began. The first step was the nationalization of commerce. Most goods were seized and sent to the Soviet Union. Next, zloty, the Polish currency, whose prewar value had been twenty rubles, was reduced to one ruble and then withdrawn altogether. People had to face the catastrophe of losing all their savings.

For a few weeks, stores were closed. The only food we could get was from nearby farms, but gradually some stores reopened. These were now government stores. Under the new law, the farmers had to sell their products to big, official warehouses and from there the food was distributed to the city stores. The result was that the whole process took so long; many perishable items were spoiled by the time they reached consumers.

Every morning big lines formed for bread, milk and scarce food items. It sometimes took several hours to get something. Products of even the most elementary kind became unobtainable. Rigidly controlled state-owned shops, when they had anything to sell at all, seldom had what consumers required. Only that which the State cared to furnish was available.

Eventually the peasants were urged to pool their own holdings and start farming on collective farms. The change in lifestyle was so drastic that it was almost impossible to comprehend this reality. The standard of living for everyone, even the poorest, was falling at a running speed to a point far below anything believed possible, and as the Western borders were now sealed, one had the impression of being in a large prison with the NKVD as the prison guards.

The occupied territory was annexed completely to the Soviet Union, and administered by Soviet officials. They were in all the top positions. In time, more and more bureaucrats with their families came from the Soviet Union.

Our house was nationalized. In Stalin's society, personal property such as houses was not allowed. We could keep only two rooms. These were my former bedroom and my parent's bedroom—two adjoining rooms with a connecting door—and as we bought a lock for the hallway, it became like a small apartment.

Two Soviet families moved in. One family took father's study and our dining room. The other occupied the living room and my sister's former bedroom, which was next to mine. We all had to use the same kitchen and bathroom.

One family consisted of a man and wife in their thirties with two small children. The man, raised on party teachings, was full of slogans. Constantly quoting Marx, Engels, Lenin, and Stalin, he resembled a computer programmed to do his work blindly, with no questions asked. The woman seemed rather simple and quiet, fully devoted to her children.

The other family was just a couple. His job, connected with collectivization of the farms, often took him out of town. When I met Natasha, his wife, I really liked her. She was a very good-looking woman in her late twenties, a little more than medium height, with red hair, green eyes, and a slightly plump figure.

These people were the product of a system where Stalin and his party were almighty. Crawling before authorities and constant fear were a way of life. Still, Natasha seemed to be a happy, outgoing woman who liked to laugh and sing. When her husband was out of town, she would come and visit us in our part of the house. At first she was apprehensive about talking openly, but gradually we learned that her parents were rich farmers in the Ukraine. In 1932 they resisted compulsory collectivization and were deported to Siberia along with her fifteen-year-old sister. Natasha never heard of them again.

4   SCHOOL

S ince schools were about to open, mother applied for a job as a schoolteacher. Father had changed drastically. He used to be always happy, full of energy, a brilliant lawyer. He liked people and everybody liked him. His exceptional honesty was well known. I called him a "factory of jokes" because he always had something funny to say.

Now father was withdrawn, always gloomy, and suddenly aged despite his forty-seven years. Even his best friend, the judge, could not help him out of his depression.

"Life is over," father was saying. "All my family perished during the revolution, and now it's my turn."

I overheard him asking the judge to take care of mother and me in case of his arrest. Neither father nor the judge applied for a job. "Stalin's justice is not my kind of justice," father said, and the judge added, "The only person I would like to prosecute is Stalin himself. It's a pity there is no punishment big enough for his crimes."

Finally, at the end of October, schools opened. We had the same teachers, but the principal was a Soviet official dressed in a uniform. He was a stocky man in his forties with the face of a peasant. After a couple of days, all students were assembled in our main hall to greet the new principal. He started his speech with the statement that we all should be very happy and grateful that we were now under the protection of Stalin and the Communist Party. We would have to be loyal and obey them solemnly. "Look at me," he said. "I murdered a man in a brawl, but I joined the Party, and the Party forgave me, and now I am a very important man." The speech lasted a long time on the same subject, the praise of Stalin.

Besides the principal, there were five Soviet so-called political advisers and instructors. Their duty was to indoctrinate students into Lenin-Stalin ideology. One hour a day was devoted to Party teaching and political enlightenment. Special commissaries were appointed for the propagation of atheism throughout the school. We were taught that it was our duty to report everything we heard said against the system, even if it involved our parents, relatives or friends.

This new teaching clashed drastically with my inbred beliefs of duty and honor. It sounded monstrous to me. I felt lost, more so than my friend and dearest ally, Tonia.

Tonia and I had become friends when I first started school, and all these years we were almost inseparable. We were very different in nature, but I do not remember that we ever had a quarrel. Tonia was a beautiful girl with long, dark, wavy hair and violet-blue eyes. We were the same height and build, but I was rather quiet and shy, and Tonia was full of life and sparkle.

In January, Tonia turned sixteen. Being two years older than I, she always acted protectively towards me. Her parents owned a large estate west of town and had a small house in the city where they spent winter months so that Tonia and her brother could attend school. Her brother, little Andrei, was eleven, a rather sickly child. He took after his mother, a tall and slender woman with sad eyes, who, after rheumatic fever in her childhood, always had problems with her health. Tonia was a copy of her father—healthy, bubbly, always in some kind of mischief. Since she was fifteen, many boys courted her and she flirted right and left. She often said, "A respectable girl has to have several slaves around." At that time, flirting was very innocent. It was a game of smiles, eye contact, jokes, teasing and insinuations, but no touching. A boy had to court a girl for a long time before he could dream of attempting a kiss. Kissing was very risky business.

Since summer, Vasia was in the rank of Tonia's "slaves." When Germany started the war, Tonia's father, being a reserve officer of the Polish army, was drafted and sent to the Western front. Before the borders were sealed off, he managed to relate the news to his family that he was alive and in Warsaw under German occupation.

Soon their estate was nationalized and the family moved into town. Despite all the hardship, Tonia tried to be her old, cheerful self. She took all the drastic changes probably better than I did. "Well, life has to go on, and we are still young, Lara, we have to try to make the best of it."

5   LIFE GOES ON

The end of November 1939 brought an unusual amount of snow and record low temperatures. Quite often it plunged below minus thirty degrees Fahrenheit. We were already used to being in two rooms. They were easy to heat even with the scarcity of wood. My parents' bedroom remained intact, but my room was converted into living quarters since it was a big room. In the middle we put the dining table, at the wall was my piano and dresser, my desk was under the window. Instead of my bed, I now had a nice couch, which opened into a double bed. Sometimes Tonia stayed overnight and the bed was big enough for both of us. Now I was learning how to cook, wash and clean, and I was happy I could help.

Also in November, a music school opened. It was run by the Soviets. The director of the school was a woman from the Soviet Ukrainian Republic. She was in her late forties, with grayish hair and big, brown eyes. She took me as a student, and I valued her teaching very much. She was pleasant, kind, and knowledgeable; a good pianist and teacher.

It seemed that music and dance were less rigidly controlled by the state. These were the domains where people could express themselves more freely, and it flourished. There were many good musicians, brilliant pianists, violinists, singers and dancers in the Soviet Union. Trying to impress the occupied population, the officials were bringing to our town many quality shows and concerts. Especially beautiful were the folklore performances — so colorful and executed to perfection. I attended as many performances as possible. Sometimes I went with mother, sometimes with Tonia, and very often Vasia would join us.

Tonia tolerated Vasia's courtship with a smile. "Vasia, you are not a knight on a white horse and that is what I am waiting for," she would say.

"Tonia, you are cruel, but wait, I can get a horse. Brown, I can get easily, but if you insist on white, I assure you I will get one, too. But a knight's armor, don't you think you are asking too much?"

They teased each other a great deal.

Vasia always had many friends. With some of them he played cards once a week. His closest friend had a shortwave radio and sometimes they listened to the British broadcast together. This was extremely dangerous because only official communiqués were allowed. But at least once in a while we had undistorted news about what was happening in the world. But the world was about to change.

6 STALIN INVADES FINLAND

O n the last day in November, 1939, Vasia brought us news that the Red Army had invaded Finland. After occupying our part of Poland, Stalin exerted pressure on the Baltic States—Estonia, Latvia and Lithuania—and they succumbed. But Finland refused to yield to the Soviet's sweeping demands, and in spite of two months of constant pressure and threats, Stalin could not force the Finns to surrender. On November 30th he used force.

There was no declaration of war. The huge mass of tanks, artillery, machine guns and warplanes began to surge forward. Stalin was copying Hitler's campaign in Poland, but the Finns knew that Soviet victory would mean death and slavery, and they decided to fight, whatever the cost, regardless of the odds. The Mannerheim Line—a zone twenty miles deep running diagonally across the Karelian Isthmus—was strongly fortified. The Finns also had elaborate systems of booby traps and mines. The soldiers, although small in numbers, were highly trained and skilled. They fought on skis in familiar territories, and what they lacked in equipment they compensated in courage and resourcefulness. The Red Army was stopped and driven back with appalling slaughter.

In the third week of December, the Finns launched an offensive. This beat back the Soviet forces some distance and threw the enemy into confusion. No further attacks against the Mannerheim Line could be foreseeable in the near future. There were rumors of possible British and French intervention. That raised our hopes as well, because our own freedom was possible only with outside help. But we waited in vain. None of the Western countries came to our aid.

7   ARRESTS

We felt the grip of terror even more since mass arrests began in earnest before Christmas. In the first wave, father's old friend, the judge, was arrested. That was a big shock for my father. The two men had known each other for twenty years and there was a strong bond between them. Father knew that sooner or later he too would be arrested. Although the position of a judge was more prestigious than that of a lawyer, as a Russian émigré, he couldn't escape the same fate. I remembered the judge's words, "For Stalin, you are a runaway slave."

The arrests were political, always done in the middle of the night without any warning. There would be a knock on the door and NKVD soldiers would come and take the victim. First of all, former Polish officers and those who occupied any sort of noteworthy office in Polish government or public administration were arrested, then clergy, big estate owners, and simply those who in the eyes of the NKVD were considered socially dangerous. Some were released after three or four days of interrogations. The nature of the interrogations remained secret, and those released never talked about what happened to them. Others simply vanished because there never was an open-court procedure. Their crimes were labeled "capitalistic exploitation of the masses" and punished by death or hard labor in Siberia. The judge must have belonged to this last category because even his only daughter could not get any news of his whereabouts. Her's was a devastating case since her mother had been buried two years earlier.

Nobody felt safe. Even if two friends met on the street they would try to avoid each other. The NKVD had spies and informers everywhere. People went to bed at night not knowing if they would wake up under the same roof. Even slight expressions of malcontent were dangerous. At school, students eyed each other with suspicion. I had always had many friends before, but now I could talk openly only to Tonia.

8 CHRISTMAS

Christmas was approaching. It was always such a delightful time, with church services, Christmas-tree decorating, singing Christmas carols, and parties. Now churches were closed. Christmas Day was just another day on the calendar, and unless it coincided with Sunday, was a working day. Soviet society celebrated only the New Year.

When I was eight years old, father planted a pine tree in front of our house. Now it was quite tall. Every year I would decorate it with snowballs and icicles I had gathered from the awnings, and because it was always covered with snow I called it my White Christmas tree. This year it stood simply covered with snow. I cut a branch off the tree and put it in a vase on my desk. I felt so depressed. There was little vitality left for looking into the future. Practically, it was impossible to plan anything ahead, and all one could do was to keep on existing. Most time was wasted standing in lines for food and other necessities. Energy was devoted to mere survival. But there were some special stores, well concealed and well supplied, that catered exclusively to NKVD and other top Soviet officials. The rest of the Soviet bureaucrats had to stand in lines like we did, and they probably were just as afraid as we were of the almighty NKVD.

Christmas came and went almost unnoticed. Tonia stayed with her family, I with mine. I asked her to join us, but she declined.

"Well, I better stay with mama and Andrei. Mama won't go anywhere. It is the first Christmas without father, and we miss him. But I am glad he is not here. As a Polish officer, he surely would have been arrested."

She was right. In the years to come, we learned that in the year 1940 alone, and by Stalin's direct order, twenty-thousand Polish officers were massacred in Katyn.

I noticed some periods of depression even in Tonia, but they were short and she would soon perk up again. "We have to be strong, Lara, strong no matter what," she would say. I was deeply attached to her. She was my dearest friend. I tried so so badly to believe her.

9   MY BIRTHDAY

New Year was coming and so was my fifteenth birthday. I was born on the thirty-first of December, but my parents always gave me a big party on New Year's Day.

"Lara, we have to celebrate your birthday somehow," mother said.

It seemed strange even to me to think about having fun. I looked at my mother, noticing how much she had aged. There were strands of white hair at her temples and deep wrinkles around her mouth and eyes. Always strong and energetic, she liked parties and was happy with a house full of guests. Now, since the occupation, as father was in a constant state of depression, the decisions of life rested on her shoulders. She was the only breadwinner, working as a teacher. I helped as much as I could, standing in lines, cooking and cleaning. I really did not want any festivities for my birthday, but Tonia decided otherwise.

"Nonsense, Lara, of course we have to have some kind of party, even a small one. We'll just invite Vasia—at least I am going to have somebody to tease—and he can bring one of his friends."

"But, Tonia…"

"No buts. It is decided, and I volunteer to bake a cake."

"You will need butter, and you know how hard it is to get."

"I will bake without butter."

"And without sugar?"

"Don't worry about sugar. We still have a big jar of honey from the good times."

We told Vasia about our plans, and he agreed to bring a friend.

"I will invite Misha. He is not much fun, all brains, you know, but a good kid, someone we can trust."

Misha was an only son, born to his parents in their late years. He attended a private school and graduated like Vasia in June before the occupation. In October he entered a university in Lvov, which was about five-hundred miles from our city. Now he was home for the winter break.

Misha was a tall, slightly overweight boy of eighteen with brown hair and light-blue eyes. His hair was cut very short and it was not becoming. He also seemed quiet and a little bit clumsy. I met him at Vasia's several times, but I don't think we spoke two words to each other. Tonia did not know him at all, and was looking forward to meeting someone new.

"Tonia, you can practice all your charms on Misha, poor fellow," I joked.

On New Year's Eve I cleaned our modest lodging and helped mother prepare some food for tomorrow. It was very cold, almost blizzard-like. I went to bed early, but could not fall asleep. One of our neighbor's children was sick and I could heart him crying and complaining. Only a thin wall separated my room from theirs. I lay awake thinking about what was ahead. I was now fifteen. I remembered how I always wanted to be older. Did I still want that? There was nothing to look forward to.

I awoke to a beautiful day. After last night's storm the earth looked white and clean. The temperature was way below zero, but the sun was shining and the sky was a deep blue. The day passed swiftly. Vasia, his mother, and Misha were supposed to come at five o'clock. Tonia arrived a little early to help me get everything ready.

Ah, how beautiful she looked. The red dress she wore gave her complexion a special glow. Black hair framed her classical face with curls, and her violet eyes were shining and mischievous.

"Oh my. You look absolutely gorgeous, Tonia," I exclaimed.

She eyed me critically. "Don't you have anything else to wear?"

"What is wrong with what I have on now?" I had on my navy-blue dress with long sleeves and a white collar.

"But you look like a nun with those dangling braids. That's for little girls."

I refused to change the dress, but let her arrange my braids around my head like a crown.

"Now, that's much better," she said, viewing me critically. "Don't forget you're fifteen years old now, not a child anymore."

There was a knock on the door and our guests arrived. Vasia introduced Misha to Tonia. In the crowded room he looked somehow bigger and clumsier. At the beginning of the evening, Vasia and Tonia monopolized the conversation. I could see that Tonia was in a very joyful mood. Soon we set down to dinner. It felt so good to be in the company of my family and dearest friends. Even father seemed to be his old self and told a few jokes.

Misha appeared to be composed and a little bit reserved.

It was somehow strange to laugh and be happy. Time was flying by. Soon Vasia's mother left and my parents retired to their bedroom. So the four of us decided to play cards. As usual, Vasia was cheating, and the rest of us were trying to catch him. I noticed that Tonia's attention was on Misha. She was teasing him and flirting with him, behaving as I had never seen her before with any other boy. Although Misha looked happy and joked, he appeared to be composed and a little bit reserved.

Mother's head appeared at the door. "Children, do you know what time it is? It's past twelve—time to go to bed."

Reluctantly, we had to part. Tonia stayed overnight, so I escorted the boys to the front door. Vasia ran quickly home, but Misha hesitated at the door.

"Lara, I am leaving in two days for college, but tomorrow there is a fine concert with pianist, Gillels, from Russia. I would be very happy if you would go with me."

His offer caught me off guard.

"I really don't know, Misha."

"Are you free tomorrow?"

"I think so, yes."

"Then it's settled. I will pick you up at five. The concert starts at six, but it is better to be early to get a decent seat. Be ready at five."

I locked the door and paused. *Was it a date? That was so unexpected. Should I go?* I really didn't give him an answer, he had decided for me.

I came back to my room. Tonia was sitting shuffling the cards. She did not look happy—her sparkle was gone.

"Tonia, anything wrong?"

She threw the cards on the table and stood up. "Funny," she said, "the first boy I liked, and all my efforts were for nothing."

"Why do you think that?" I asked the empty question.

"Because, very simply, my dear girl, he had eyes only for you."

I felt terrible. "But I didn't encourage him at all."

"I know that, and I don't blame you." She smiled at me. "Now let's go to bed. I feel exhausted."

Silently we prepared for bed. Something changed between us, and I could not stand it.

"Tonia, I have something to say."

"Could it wait until tomorrow?"

"No, I have to tell you now."

She looked at me with curiosity.

"Well, Misha asked me to go to the concert with him tomorrow night. But I won't go, of course. I'll never see him again, and I don't even like him, and... Oh, how I wish he would've asked you instead of me."

Softness appeared in Tonia's eyes.

"He invited you to the concert? That was very nice, and of course you'll go, you silly girl. I'm happy for you. It's about time you had some fun... And now, lights out. I need sleep."

In the morning Tonia was her old cheerful self, in a bright mood and teasing me about my first date.

"Promise me you'll go, or I'll never speak to you again," she said before she left.

I was nervous all day. Misha came a little before five. Immediately he put me at ease.

"Lara, it is very cold outside. Dress warmly, and off we go!" He was in a happy mood, and we joked and laughed on the way to the concert. Gillel's performance was absolutely brilliant. I had never heard a pianist of his caliber before.

"Impressed?"

"Oh, yes." I sighed. My own playing seemed so childish.

At the door, Misha held my hand for a moment. "I'm leaving tomorrow. I'll be back in June. Lara, I know what you are going through, the change of life is so drastic. But, remember, there is a lot you can do. Study, practice, read, get as much knowledge as you can. You have your music, so hold on. I'll see you in June." He squeezed my hand and ran down the steps.

"Misha, careful, the steps are icy."

He smiled and waved at me.

10 FATHER'S ARREST

In a couple of days, school was resumed after the winter break. School, homework, standing in lines, everything was just time consuming, and it was so bitterly cold this winter. In Finland, fighting became more fierce, but it was clear that the Red Army's performance, in spite of all the armor, revealed shameful weaknesses. Still the Finns knew that they could not hold on forever. Neither France nor Britain interfered.

In the middle of January there were a few more arrests. Night after night the dreaded black vans of the secret police raced through the streets, picking up their victims.

One night a loud knock woke me up. Mother appeared at the door of her room. "Lara, are you making that noise?"

I pointed to the entrance door. Somebody was banging on it. Mother ran to get a robe and opened the door. Three NKVD soldiers came in. They wanted father and showed the notice of his arrest.

"Tell your husband to get dressed and be quick about it."

Mother disappeared into her bedroom. I lay in my bed and looked with horror at the soldiers. So it happened, the dreadful arrest happened. *They are going to take father away, and I might not see him ever again.* I wished I could get up and go to the room where father was dressing, but the soldiers stood there, and I only pulled the blanket up to my nose. Father came out, already in his winter coat. He turned toward me and wanted to say something, but one of the soldiers pushed him to the front entrance.

"We don't have all night. Go." The outside door closed behind them.

Mother stood staring motionless for a moment, then turned toward me.

"I have to go to the NKVD headquarters. Maybe they'll tell me something. I can't just stay home."

"I'll go with you."

She hesitated, then said, "All right, just dress warmly."

Bone-chilling cold enveloped us. By the time we came to the huge building, we were half frozen. There were lights in the windows. Stalin's henchmen were working full time. Rudely we were told to go home and stay there for our own good. Back home, our two rooms seemed so empty and cold. I crawled into mother's bed.

"Can I, please?"

"Of course, dear."

Her face looked tired, with dark circles under her eyes. I felt as if a big hand was squeezing my throat.

"Mama, is there any hope we'll see father again?"

"I was thinking the same thing. Remember Alla? She is a couple of years older than you. Their house is across from Tonia's. Her father is also a lawyer, and he was arrested in December and released after several days. Communists cannot keep everybody in prison. Some arrests are their tactics to scare all thinking people." She paused and then added, "In Stalin's mind, he who thinks is dangerous. So let's hope and pray. That's all we can do." She drew me closer. "And now, close your eyes, little one, it's still a couple of hours until dawn."

Morning came, gray and snowy. Mother had to go to work, I to school. In the kitchen I saw Natasha.

"Do you know what happened last night?"

"Yes, I had to open the front door." She came close to me.

"Lara, I know how you feel, believe me. Remember I told you I lost my parents and my sister? She was your age then, even looked a little bit like you. But I survived, so try to be strong, dear girl."

I thanked Natasha. She was a good woman. At school the news about father's arrest spread quickly. Some of the kids started to avoid me. I did not blame them. Tonia tried to cheer me up as much as she could. Days went by without any news. Mother went again to the NKVD, and this time they told her that father was under investigation.

Finally on the sixth day, late at night, NKVD soldiers brought father home. He was a shadow of a man, face drawn, red eyes. He had lost quite a bit of weight. His hands shook when mother served him tea. He could not hold the cup. Six days, or rather nights, of constant questioning broke the poor man. He was accused of being a Czarist officer, of deserting his country when he fled to Poland, of counter-revolutionary inclinations.

"Why did you not apply for work?" He was asked. "If you are not with us, you are against us." That was one of the Communist slogans.

Finally, they let him go—for now. It was a big relief to have father home. We had to live from day to day and be satisfied and happy that we were still alive.

11   DEPORTATIONS

B y February of 1940, the Red Army was half a
million strong. Stalin began a new offensive
in Finland on the Mannerheim line. His plan
was to bring the war to a rapid and successful
conclusion. With no outside help, the poor Finns had
no chance.

February's cold seemed to become more bitter,
and it was hard to stand for hours in the food lines.
Natasha helped some. Her husband, employed in
the agricultural department, often brought produce
from his visits to the farms, and Natasha was eager
to exchange some food items for clothing. Her
belongings were very meager when she came to our
town, but, as she and mother were the same size,
her wardrobe improved substantially. She was as
delighted with every new piece of clothing as a child
with a new toy.

Sometimes at dinner we joked that today we were
eating mother's blouse, or shoes, or a scarf. I noticed

that we were getting conditioned to the new life of fear, hopelessness, and resignation, and we had to go on existing.

On February 14, around 7 o'clock in the morning, as I was getting up, someone knocked on my window. It was Tonia signaling me to let her in. She entered frozen and shaking.

"Tonia, what happened? Your mother? Andrei?"

"We're all right, but I had to be sure you were still here."

"Still here?"

"Lara, the soldiers are loading people on trucks with their belongings and taking them somewhere."

"What?"

"Our neighbors, the house across the street. Alla's father was arrested and released just like your father. I was afraid they might have taken all of you. I had to come and see if you were all right."

I noticed mother standing in the doorway listening. "Dear God," she said, "so it's happening here, too."

Mother explained to us that there were many deportations in Russia under Stalin's rule, especially in the early thirties in the Ukraine where people resisted collectivization. Thousands upon thousands of families, sometimes whole villages, were relocated to Siberia and Asiatic Russia.

"Where are the soldiers taking those people?" Tonia asked.

"Probably to railway stations to be loaded into cattle cars for the long journey east. Whoever survives these inhuman circumstances is settled in remote outposts far away from railway lines or towns, and put to work, slaving under the most severe conditions."

We listened with horror. At school everybody was whispering with fear about deportations. Some students were missing. Later on, we learned that enormous numbers of trains were assembled and waiting. Thousands of people were abducted from our town and nearby cities—men, women and children. They were allowed only thirty minutes for packing their belongings.

After entrainment, the doors and windows of the cars were locked, leaving only an opening for the provision of food and elimination of excrement.

Deportees were labeled politically and socially dangerous and included not only civil servants, landlords, officers, teachers, priests and former policemen, but even peasants and shopkeepers whose only crime was that they worked all their lives to achieve some prosperity.

Deportations took place in the worst weather anyone could remember. The complete lawlessness of this act was unthinkable for a person used to a democratic society, yet no one could do anything about it or even condemn it openly for fear of being arrested.

This time my family was spared, but we were expecting the worst and assumed there would be more deportations in the near future.

12   THE COMING OF SPRING

B y the end of February, Lent started, seven weeks before Easter. Usually, it was a period of daily special church services, moderation in food and social activities, confession of sins and communion in church. Now, without church services, we prayed at home and tried to observe Lent. Meat was scarce these days. Vasia joked, "One good thing about Lent, we don't need to stand in the meat lines."

Vasia was still supplying us with the news from the British broadcast, especially about the war in Finland. His contact with the underground radio worried his mother very much. It was so dangerous, but Vasia remained happy-go-lucky in spite of everything.

"Don't worry, mother, nobody can suspect that I am getting my information during our weekly card games."

Then one day, all four of the boys were arrested, held overnight in NKVD and told to stop their weekly gatherings. Four people meeting at regular intervals were considered in Stalin's society to be a step to conspiracy. The arrest frightened Vasia out of his wits.

I worried about father. He hardly spoke, lay moodily in bed, or sat silently in his chair. Both mother and I tried to take him for a walk everyday before dinner.

March brought a new promise of spring. Days were longer and not so cold. During our walks father was mostly quiet, deep in his thoughts, but gradually he started talking about his life in pre-Revolutionary Russia, his family and his ancestors. Sometimes I would catch his concerned look when he was gazing at me.

Once he said, "If something happens to me, I want you to be strong, Lara. You are a big girl now, and you have to take care of your mother."

I understood that he was referring to the possibility of another arrest.

I wanted to say something, but he interrupted. "Lara, whatever happens, you and mother will be better off."

"But, papa—"

"Don't say anything, just remember, you both will be better off."

In the following days, he appeared composed and calm, even joked a little bit.

On March twelfth the Soviets signed a treaty with Finland. Finns were forced to surrender the Vyborg

Isthmus and Eastern Korelia, but they could still maintain some kind of independence. Their heroic fighting was justified because Stalin's original aim was complete absorption of Finland into the Soviet system.

On the last day of March, it was my turn to take father for his afternoon walk and it was a beautiful day, full of sunshine. It felt warm, melting snow formed big puddles. I hurried home from school. Breathing deeply, I tried to fill my lungs to their capacity. The air smelled fresh with a mixture of warmth and invigorating coldness.

I'm going to take father to the river today, I thought. *Maybe the ice has already started to melt.*

The door to our rooms was wide open, which was unusual. I called to father—no answer. I went outside and looked around. Natasha was standing in her room by an open window.

"It's beautiful today, isn't it, Lara?" She said.

"Natasha, did you see my father?"

"I saw him this morning, but not after that. I just came back from town."

What is happening? I started to worry. I searched our rooms. Father's coat was in the closet. I went to the kitchen. The door to the corridor, which led to the storage area, was open. I ran inside and there on the concrete floor was my father with a torn length of rope around his neck. The other piece was hanging from the exposed beam. He was on his back, eyes closed. I touched his hand; it was warm, so was his face. I had only one thought—still alive, still alive.

I ran back to the kitchen shouting, "Natasha, help, please help." She came out of her room. "Father, there—he hung himself."

"What are you talking about, Lara? Are you out of your mind?"

"Please, Natasha, I think he is still alive."

She pushed me aside, went into the storage space and knelt beside the body, putting her ear to father's chest.

"His heart is still beating. Quick, Lara, get the doctor. I'll stay here." By the time I came with the doctor, father was moving his head and moaning.

Natasha had untied the rope from father's neck and, not without difficulty, the three of us picked him up and carried him to his bed. The doctor examined father's head carefully.

"It is a concussion." He said gravely. "He must have hit his head hard when the rope gave way. I will stay with your father, Lara, until he comes to, and you... You had better prepare your mother when she comes home."

I went to my room. Natasha was still there.

"Natasha, I don't know how to thank you." Tears filled my eyes. I came close to her, wishing to embrace her. She stopped me.

"Don't fall apart, girl. Get a hold of yourself." Her voice was stern and dry. "There are worse things than that." She shook her head. "You Westerners, you're all weaklings. You can't face harsh reality. I'll go and untie the other piece of the rope from the beam. Don't tell anyone what happened. It's better that way."

"Don't tell anyone about what? And what rope to untie?"

Mother stood in the doorway. Fear was in her eyes. She heard Natasha's last sentences.

Natasha left abruptly, and I told mama everything that happened. She rushed to the next room. For a long time I sat exhausted on the couch. I heard mother's and the doctor's voices. Soon, I distinguished father's voice as well. I had to see him.

Father was propped up on two pillows, his face pale and drawn.

"Lara, please forgive me. I..."

"Papa," I interrupted. "It's all right, it's all right. The main thing is you're alive."

In the days to follow, we talked a lot. I had to understand many things. Father explained that with him gone, he hoped the communist authorities would leave mama and me alone. It was so hard for him to remain silent and submissive with all the lawlessness surrounding us. Suicide was his way of denouncing Stalin's rule, and should he be arrested again, he feared reprisals against mother and me.

I learned that in April 1935, Stalin issued a decree making children from the age of twelve and on subject to criminal and political charges and to adult treatment, including the penalty of death. Father wanted to spare me this horrible punishment.

During 1937, there were mass arrests in the Soviet Union as Stalin was getting rid of Lenin's so-called Old Guard. These were idealistic revolutionaries whom he greatly feared. Reprisals against children, wives and parents were used as a method of breaking the morale of political prisoners and making them confess whatever the interrogators wanted them to admit.

In the case of an arrest, not only did the immediate family suffer, but also friends, acquaintances, and even persons with whom the arrested had been in contact. Other arrests followed. Labor camps had to be filled with a free work force to complete Stalin's grandiose plans for socioeconomic and industrial development. I understood father and he was not a weakling. Suicide for him was an honorable way out without endangering those closest to him, but we made him promise no further attempts at self-destruction for mine and mother's sake.

Now thoughts of ending my own life started to haunt me. What kind of life lay ahead? Constant fear, watching every word, suppressing real feelings, complete submission, and most of all, the necessity of applauding and praising the worst villain in the world—the one who was responsible for the deaths of incalculable numbers of victims. Was this a life worth living?

I shared my thoughts with Tonia.

"Oh, my God," she said. "Now I will have to worry about you even more. Put those stupid ideas out of your mind right now. Let us live just a day at a time. That is all we can do, Lara. Don't you think that it has to stop someday? It's so beautiful outside, let's go for a long walk."

"Dear, dear Tonia, what would I do without you?"

13   THE NEW TENANT

Easter was approaching, the resurrection of Jesus Christ, the promise of life everlasting. In previous years, preparation for Easter started during Lent. I liked the church services, they were full of spirituality, beautiful prayers and songs. I especially liked the last week before Easter. On Thursday night we listened to the reading of the twelve Gospels, and brought lighted candles home. At the Easter midnight service, the church was adorned with flowers, aglow with candlelight as the priest triumphantly exclaimed, time and time again, *Christ has risen*. And we answered, *Indeed, He's risen*, a tradition entrenched in the souls of Russian people for centuries. This proud tradition Stalin would erase.

At the beginning of April we learned that the Soviet family with two children who occupied the front rooms of our house suddenly had to move. They were not happy about it, but one of the NKVD high officials liked our home and simply told them to get out.

"Can he do that?" I asked Natasha.

"You're still very naive, Lara," she said.

"But if they would complain?"

"To whom? And besides, they wouldn't dare. He works in the NKVD."

So in a week or so we had a new tenant. He was a man in his late thirties, about six feet tall, very muscular, with a rather handsome face were it not for a pair of unpleasant, piercing dark eyes. The first time I saw him I took an instant dislike. He had a wife and daughter in the Soviet Union. They were supposed to join him after the school term ended.

He occupied my sister's bedroom, and only a thin wall separated my room from his. Since he worked nights, I often heard him come home late and wondered who his victim was that night. Years ago it would have been impossible to believe that one of Stalin's men would live in our house.

In compensation, it seemed, for the long, cold winter, April brought sunshine and very warm temperatures. The snow had already melted, the first flowers appeared, and trees were dressing themselves in delicate green foliage.

On Easter Day our small group gathered together: Tonia's family, my family, Vasia and his mother. We even had colored eggs, although there were only two colors—brown and light green. Food coloring was impossible to buy and we obtained the brown color by cooking eggs with onion skins, the green, by using fresh birch leaves.

Our Easter table was modest, and we were almost silent as we sampled our food. We could hear the NKVD man moving behind the wall. It was a sad Easter. Even Vasia was depressed, and there was none of the usual bickering between him and Tonia.

This particular Easter remains memorable to me for another reason. This was when I first met Grisha. Grisha was Tonia's new boyfriend. What a handsome boy, medium tall, dark blond hair and gray eyes. He always seemed to be nervous and tense.

Grisha had lived in a nearby town with his parents and two younger sisters. In February, while he was visiting his elderly aunt in our town, his whole family was deported to the Soviet Union. He was left behind, and since the authorities didn't know what to do with him, he simply stayed with his aunt.

He was terribly sad. "Until the next deportation," he used to say, gloomily.

Even though I was sad too, I was secretly happy, because he joined our school. Tonia too felt sorry for him and tried to help him cope with his grief. Soon they became close friends. He hardly noticed me.

14   ANOTHER DEPORTATION

A t the end of April, scary rumors started to circulate in our town. Large gatherings of cattle wagons were spotted on the back tracks of the railway station. Another deportation? The first time it was done without warning, but now, as no one was really safe, many started to pack ahead of time. We, too, prepared two suitcases of imperishable food and warm clothing. So far there was no news about the people who had been deported in February. What happened to them, where they were, even their relatives did not know.

In spite of everything, I studied hard at school, doing my homework, reading, practicing the piano, trying just not to think. I repeated Misha's words, *Get as much knowledge as you can, Lara.*

Life continued thus, until one morning I was awakened by the grating sound of a noisy truck motor. It was barely dawn. I listened for a while. *The noise is steady. The truck is stationary,* I thought.

But *the motor is not shut off.* Soviet trucks were exceedingly noisy. I put on my robe and ran to the front door. Through the glass I could see a truck in front of our house. Four soldiers were standing by it. They seemed to look around, then two of them opened our gate and started to ascend the stairs. "So this is it," I whispered, "deportation."

I watched the soldiers come up and open the door without knocking. They stared at me, startled. "What number is this house?" One of them asked. I felt my lips move, but did not hear my voice.

"Louder, speak up."

"Nineteen."

"Oh!" His eyes seemed to narrow. "Twenty. Where is it?"

"I don't know."

The soldiers turned around and ran down the steps. Drained, I stood in the doorway. Soon the soldiers were knocking at the door of a house across the street. A young woman with a five-year-old daughter lived there. Little Mary looked like a doll—blond hair, blue eyes. The thought raced through my mind: *why would the Soviets deport a woman and child?* They were of modest means. Maybe because the husband was a Polish officer? Several Polish military families were deported in February, but Mary's father was never there. After the short war he remained in Germany, just like Tonia's father. *Oh, my God, it's just like Tonia's family.* I felt chilled from top to toe. The possibility of their deportation was unbearable. In my room I dressed feverishly. *Hurry, Lara, it's already past six. Mother and father are still sleeping. I should write a note, just a couple of words. I must see Tonia. That's it, now go!*

I walked rapidly, breathing heavily. The air was fresh, even crisp. I knew that sooner or later my parents and I would be deported, but not Tonia. A sick woman, small boy and a seventeen-year-old girl… None of them was strong enough to work in a harsh, remote frontier. *Oh, Lara,* I thought, *you panic so easily and are crazy to be rushing like this. Tonia is probably fast asleep. If you wake her up she will be mad at you, and she will say, "Look at that silly girl. She deprives me of a whole half-hour of sleep and worries herself sick. What am I going to do with you?" But I will be so relieved and happy.*

A couple of trucks loaded with people and guarded by soldiers passed me.

As soon as I turned to Tonia's street I saw the truck in front of her house. Tonia's mother and brother were already inside and Tonia was standing beside it handing them packages. I started running as fast as I could. By the time I reached the truck, Tonia had already climbed in and soldiers were closing the tailgate.

"Tonia!" I wanted to reach to her, but one of the soldiers pushed me back. I fell to the sidewalk. When I got up, the truck started rolling. Tonia waved to me. She said something but I could not understand it. Her face was stern and solemn. She kept waving softly with her right hand. In a moment the truck disappeared around the corner.

I felt as if something ripped open inside me. *NO, NO, NO*, a voice was crying in my mind. *No, you can't take my dear friend away.* Frantically, I paced the sidewalk. Hatred was filling deep inside—hatred of Stalin and his cursed system. I wished for once, I could just shout it out. For once, say what I felt.

Now, Lara, get a hold of yourself. Nothing you can do, no one can. You are alone now. But how am I going to face this new ordeal?

Then Natasha's harsh words flashed through my mind, "You Westerners are all weaklings."

The door to the house was open. I went up and closed it and sat on the doorstep. The sun was up and its rays should have felt warm. *At least it's not cold and summer is coming.* In the garden some flowers were already blooming. They looked cold to me too. The earth was swelling with new life. I couldn't bear the thought of the suffering in store for my friend. I put my head on my knees. *I should go home. Yes, I will in a moment. Oh, dear God, it hurts too much.*

Someone touched my shoulder. I lifted my head. Grisha was standing in front of me. His eyes were like needles. "My family was taken and now Tonia's." He shook his fists. Choking with emotion, he almost shouted, "Someday, someday Stalin will pay for all his crimes. He will, I assure you. He must be destroyed. I only wish I could put my hand to that."

"Grisha, stop—someone might hear you."

"So be it. I don't care. I don't care to live like this. I am sick and tired of watching my every word." Suddenly he calmed down. "Let us go home, Lara. It is not easy for you, either."

Silently we walked for a couple of blocks. On the corner where we had to go our separate ways, I asked him, "How did you know Tonia would be deported?"

"I didn't. Yesterday my aunt got a letter from my parents and I wanted to share the news with Tonia before school. On my way, I understood that another deportation was in progress, and then I saw you curled up on the steps."

"You got a letter from…?"

"Yes, from Kazakstan—that's where they landed."

"Your sisters?"

"They all survived. There is not much in the letter, just asking about my whereabouts and to send them some packages."

"So, it is possible to mail something there?"

"I don't know, but we will try." Abruptly he said, "I've got to go."

Slowly, I walked home. It was easier for me now. Tonia could write, and I could help her. I thanked God for this news. *Just let Tonia and her family survive.* I prayed.

The whole morning, trucks were racing through the town and countryside. Thousands were packed into the cattle wagons. This time many were from the rural area, mostly well-to-do farmers. It was done to stamp out any thought of resistance to their hideous plans—the future collectivization of the land. In the weeks to come, there were a few straggling letters from what became known as the *February deportees.*

Letters were composed very carefully. One woman wrote that her husband went to live with his brother (deceased five years ago), and in another letter children wrote, "mama decided not to stay with us."

It would be many long years before we would learn the fate of most of these people, our heretofore friends and neighbors. Approximately one-third did not survive the long journey. The hardest hit were little children.

15 LESSON IN HISTORY

A new chapter started in my life. I realized how much I depended on my friend, Tonia. Now I could only pray that God would give her the strength to survive. Something hardened inside me. I had to deal with my problems alone. I did not want to worry my parents, so I tried to appear calm and in control.

Automatically, I did my schoolwork and practiced on the piano, but the train, going east, was constantly on my mind. I thought about all those deported in the last twenty years—those in prison, tortured and executed, and those slowly dying in labor camps. Millions suffering—all victims of Josef Stalin's tyranny! A cruel experiment was being forced upon Russia and other nations. What led to it? I had so much to understand.

During my walks with father, we talked freely. He tried to explain history to a fifteen-year-old in the simplest way. Russia, situated east, was the most backward European country. There were Asiatic influences resulting from three-hundred years of Tartar supremacy. Until Peter the Great (1672-1725), the slowly seeping influences of Western European civilization had little effect on Russia as a nation. It was Czar Peter who westernized Russian life, bringing good but drastic changes and raising the country to the rank of a great power. The succeeding rulers kept ties with the West, and were more humane, educated, and brought more culture.

In the 19th century, literature, art, music, and the theater blossomed. Philosophy and science were developing. Slavery was abolished, but still many reforms were needed. Peasants were ignorant, illiterate and poor, underpaid and barely surviving. The aristocracy and rich upper classes, with their lavish lifestyle, cared mostly about their own well-being. In the latter part of the 19th century, groups of intellectuals formed in opposition to the king, but they were suppressed.

The 20th century brought much unrest. Czar Nicolas II was a weak ruler. There were several good minds around and given time, Russia probably would have evolved gradually towards democracy. Some good agrarian reforms introduced by Stolypin were already in progress, but Stolypin was assassinated by terrorists.

In the middle of the 19th century two German writers, Marx and Engels, published their work, *Communist Manifesto*. They called on workers of all countries to unite against "capitalist oppression." A revolutionary movement was founded. It united many socialist groups, one of them being the communists, which sought to seize power by revolution. It demanded government ownership of industry and agriculture.

The Marx-Engels idea made little progress in Western Europe, but appealed to many people in Russia who worked for social reforms. One of those people was a man named Lenin. He intended to destroy the monarchy by violence and abolish private property. He attempted an unsuccessful revolution in 1905. But in November 1917, aided by conditions resulting from the war with Germany, Lenin and his followers overthrew the Russian government. Lenin became dictator of the Soviet Union and was paving the road to socialism and communism.

But old Russia would not die without a fight. Civil war broke out. Until 1921 the White Guard fought bravely, defending mother Russia against the red flag, but in the end, the communists won.

Destruction of upper and middle classes was enormous. Civil war and the effort to put communist ideas into practice brought the country near economic collapse. Russia plunged into poverty and hunger.

The living conditions in Russia were so bad that Lenin had no choice but to introduce limited free enterprise with what became known as the *New Economic Policy*. These concessions for private enterprise revived Russia, and for a time the economy improved. But Lenin was a sick man, and he died in January 1924. For Stalin, who worked closely with Lenin, that was the most opportune time to seize power.

Stalin, of Georgian descent, was a short man with a pockmarked face and yellow eyes. He was temperamental, wily and vindictive. In old Russia as a young man, he joined Lenin's Bolshevik faction and became a member of the outlawed Central Committee. He was busy in the underground organizing bank and government payroll robberies to supply the communist treasury. After the revolution, in 1922, Stalin was invited to run the Party Secretariat and he skillfully used any situation to move towards the top. Stalin's power was growing steadily, and after Lenin's death he was strong enough to act on his own. By 1929, through elimination of all opponents, he erected a government responsible to him alone. His aim was to industrialize the country by all possible means. Suddenly, without preparation, he launched mass collectivization of the land and used force to execute his plan.

For a peasant to move off his land, or part with any corner of it of his own free will was worse than parting with his own life. Peasants resisted with all their strength, but Stalin crushed the resistance with arrests and deportations. Sometimes entire villages were deported to Siberia. The result was a great famine in the Ukraine, which had been the most fertile region of the country. Millions starved and survivors were herded into collective farms, called Kalkhozes.

Some top communists opposed these harsh methods, but they too, vanished into the already established labor camps. In order to use violence effectively against the whole nation, Stalin needed a strong, obedient police force. The police force was organized by him down to the smallest detail and stretched to the remotest corner of the empire. Those on top were unscrupulous, poorly educated, morally degenerate, and completely devoted to himself. This police force was called the NKVD. It was a million strong and became Stalin's personal security organ.

Still, Stalin needed to eliminate any opposition to his political machine—the Politburo. There was conflict brewing between him and Kirov, a young party official who grew up after the revolution. My father believed Kirov was murdered on the first day of December, 1934, and the day after his death the great purges were launched. These purges were, in fact, the removal of any opposition and every vestige of collective leadership.

The Politburo, which could form the majority against Stalin, had to be neutralized. Thousands of lower and middle rank party officials went to forced labor camps. Free labor was needed to fulfill Stalin's industrial plans. Mass arrests, executions, and deportations were common practice. But the worst years were 1936-1937. Now leaders of the revolution, high party members together with a number of senior army officers, were accused and tried in public, show trials, and under pressure, confessed to unimaginable crimes. Stalin accused them of being spies for the Western countries and traitors who deserved to be shot without mercy. What harsh methods made these victims publicly confess to nonexistent crime we will never know. With the top party members toppled, many others were shot or sent to camps. It was like a chain reaction. If your friend was arrested, you too, feared arrest. In Stalin's mind, guilt or innocence was irrelevant: better a hundred innocent men in jail than one guilty person free.

People were imprisoned without cause. Mass terror, the extortion of confessions and the killing of opponents presented no ethical problem for the Red monster. At the same time, radio and newspapers described Stalin as the genius of the new world, the wisest man of the era, and the greatest leader of communism.

When the purges were over, only Stalin was left from among those who sat in Lenin's Politburo, and at the top there was now a set of blindly faithful yes-men who were drilled into absolute spiritual subjection to Stalin.

With all that I learned from father, it was easier for me to understand what was happening in the occupied territories. We all had to feel the master's whip.

16   THE NKVD MAN

It was May, warm, sunny, trees in full foliage, flowers in bloom. I lived a day at a time missing my dear friend with all my heart. Nights were hard. In the evening I would fall asleep quickly, but around 2 or 3 o'clock in the morning the noise in the adjoining room would waken me. The NKVD man, returning from his gruesome work, would not even bother to be quiet.

I hated this man and was afraid him. And worst of all, he tried to be friendly to me. For the whole of last month he seemed to be always in my path. I tried to go past him, but he stopped me.

"Wait, girl, what is the rush? Tell me, how is your school? Do you have good grades?"

"I am trying the best I can."

"Good, good, and you play the piano quite well."

"If I am bothering you with my practice, I am sorry."

"No, no, not at all. I like music, but you always play classical things. I prefer Russian or Ukrainian songs, they are so beautiful. Will you play for me? I love to sing."

The thought of having any social contact with the NKVD man was repulsive. I did not answer and rushed to my room. Often, coming from school, I would find him sitting on the balcony. He tried to engage me in conversation. He acted friendly, but I felt extremely uncomfortable under his piercing eyes. What did this man want from me?

Once as I helped mother in the kitchen, and Natasha had come out from her room to chat, the NKVD man arrived with a sack of canned goods.

"Here," he said cheerfully. "It's a treat for you." He pulled out a couple of items and gave them to Natasha, then turned and gave the sack to mother.

Natasha was reading the labels on the packages. "Sardines, dry pea soup, herring, pickled herring, smoked fish. Thank you, oh, thank you." She gushed.

Mother stood silently with the sack in her hands. "Thank you," she said finally, "but you really shouldn't have. We have everything we need."

"Oh, this is nothing, I can get you some more in the future," he boasted.

He made a couple of steps towards me. "Lara, you would like some of these goodies, I'm sure." He touched my cheek. I must have shuddered. "You're so pale, girl. We have to put some color in your cheeks." I took a step back. "There's a jar of caviar in the sack. Have you ever tasted caviar?" He was still looking at me. Words failed me. I shook my head. "And some chocolate, too."

"And one for me?" Natasha teased.

He winked at her. "Next time, I promise. But now I have to go or I'll be late for work." He waved and left.

For a moment there was silence, then mother put the sack on the table. "We cannot accept this."

"All this food is from special NKVD stores," I said.

"So what? You can't reject his gift; it is too dangerous. Are you crazy? Don't you know what power he has?" Natasha said.

"We can't. Please, Natasha, take it and don't say we gave it to you. So you see, he's not going to know. I hope you understand." Mother's voice was firm.

Natasha sighed and shook her head. "When are you going to learn to adjust?" She took the sack. "It's plain stupid to reject all these delicacies. At least take something."

"No," we said in unison.

Natasha shrugged her shoulders and left. As usual I told Tonia everything.

"It's good that you didn't accept his presents. I don't think I could swallow anything from these privileged stores. But, Lara, stay away from this man. He shows too much interest in you. I don't like it."

"But what can I do? Lately he is almost always at the front door when I come home from school."

"Take the back path and go through the storage or kitchen door," Tonia advised.

"Oh, yes, good. Why didn't I think of that?"

From the back of the house was a hill, and there was a path from another street. It was steep and slippery, but that was a good idea. Tonia always knew what to do.

But then came the deportation, and Tonia was gone from my life. I felt as if there were physical wounds inside me and resentment against the NKVD man augmented to a higher pitch. In spite of coming home through the back door, it was impossible to avoid him entirely. All I could do was run away at the first sight of him. Sometimes I would encounter his angry gaze.

It was the middle of May, and four more weeks of school remained. The common grief which Grisha and I shared developed into friendship.

Quite often we walked home from school together. He lived only a few blocks away and we could talk openly in quiet voices. He seemed to be more jittery and nervous than before.

"You know, Lara," he said to me once, "I simply can't accept what is happening. We're treated like animals. Some are taken for slaughter, some left in the pasture until... And we respond like obedient cattle."

"But what can we do except, of course, commit suicide in protest?" A picture of my father with the rope around his neck flashed into my mind.

"There's something I intend to do," Grisha lowered his voice to almost a whisper. "I want to organize an underground resistance."

I looked at him startled. "With all these hordes of NKVD and spies around us?"

"Just listen, Lara. Recently, I met some Jewish people who fled from the part of Poland under German occupation. By the way, do you know that Germans put all Jews in ghettos, and each of them has to wear a yellow insignia? I think its terrible. They told me that there is an underground Polish army, and it's well organized. So why not establish one here?"

"It's too dangerous," I said. But the idea was very appealing.

"Dangerous, dangerous? Don't be silly. What do I have to lose? You know very well that sooner or later... but at least before I die, I will take a couple of those NKVD butchers with me!"

"You mean kill?" I asked with horror.

He shrugged his shoulders. "They are killing us."

We walked silently for a while. Grisha seemed to be lost in his thoughts. He was walking so fast now that I could hardly catch up with him. I tugged at his sleeve. "Could you please slow down?"

He stopped and looked at me as if he saw me for the first time in his life, and then started walking slower.

"I shouldn't have told you all this, I shouldn't. But I had to talk to someone I can trust."

"Oh, Grisha, I'm so glad you confided in me, and I understand. Please, I want to join and participate. I want to be in the resistance, too," I pleaded.

"No, not you, not you. And anyway, you are too young." His voice was firm. "Please forget everything I told you."

We stopped at the gate to my house. Grisha took my hand and stroked it a couple of times. "Oh, Lara, it's just a thought, just a dream." He sighed. "Now go home, and not a word to anyone." He squeezed my hand and left.

Slowly I ascended the steps. On the balcony I stopped and turned around. The view was spectacular with the river like a ribbon, and Lubart Castle surrounded by green meadows. I saw blue skies, gentle rays of sunlight and blooming lilacs. I filled my lungs with the scented air. *Dear God, how beautiful,* I thought, *and how painful life is.*

When I opened the door to the house I found myself face to face with the NKVD man. His face was flushed and angry. I made a move to run, but he grabbed my hand and pulled me into the hall.

"So you have a boyfriend now, and he walks you home every day," he hissed.

I was so startled that I could only murmur, "He's not my boyfriend. He's just a friend from school." Suddenly anger filled me. "What is it to you? How dare you? Let go of my hand!" I tried to pull my hand from his grip, but he grabbed my other hand. I backed to the wall.

"What is it to me? I'll tell what it is to me. You drive me crazy. I can't think of anything but you. I can't sleep knowing you are behind the thin wall — you, so young, so desirable, so innocent."

His face was so close to mine, he almost whispered in my ear. "I want you, understand? I want you. Some night you will have to come to my room."

Pinned to the wall, I felt nauseated. "Let me go, let me go." I tried to push him away.

"Listen, girl," he changed the tone of his voice. "Don't be stupid. I can help you and your parents, too. I can protect you. I can get you anything you want, but you have to be nice to me. Don't fight me."

Abruptly he let me go. "I have to go now," he said. "But think about what I've told you. I'll be expecting you."

He went outside and slammed the door behind him.

Horrified, I stood motionless. Everything was quiet in the house. *Good, nobody is home,* I said to myself. Quickly I went to our part of the house, unlocked the door, came in, locked the door, dropped my books on the desk, and curled up on the couch, trying to make myself small and insignificant—it was easier to think in this position. I was not so naive that I didn't understand what the man proposed, but it was so horrible to me that I dismissed it instantly.

In every young girl's heart is an image of an ideal man, romance, unending love, marriage, and a happy life thereafter. Tonia and I often talked about our dreams. Now I felt like a wounded animal. *The way out—think, Lara, what is the way out?* The only way out for me was to hide for the next few weeks until the NKVD man's wife came to join him. I would go from school directly to my music school and practice there.

Mama knew that I was rehearsing the Mendelssohn concerto with my teacher. In ten days I had a big recital coming up, so I could stay there until five o'clock, the time when the NKVD man went to work. I would not be able to take father for a walk, but he was better now, and I would help mama in the evening.

"Oh, dear God," I prayed, *"if only I could talk to someone — ask for advice. If only Toni... no, no, Lara,"* I told myself, *"stop and get a hold of yourself. Don't you dare cry... You will have red eyes, and how are you going to explain that?"* The urge to cry almost overwhelmed me. *"Breathe deeply, Lara — one, two, three breathes, in and out, in and out... that's better. Now a glass of water..."*

When my parents came home, I tried to be ever so cheerful. Falling asleep that night, I prayed to God for guidance and protection. A couple of days went by uneventfully, but the noise in the NKVD man's room grew louder when he returned from work at night. Oh, how I hated him.

It was June now with only two weeks left in school. I did my school work the best I could, as if to prove that I could handle any hardship.

Sometimes Grisha walked me to the music school and we would talk about resistance. I pleaded with him to include me, but he was firm. "No girls, anyway, not your age."

On Saturdays school closed an hour earlier and the music school was open only until 3 o'clock. Mother told me in the morning that she and father would not be home in the afternoon and evening. "I have to help my friend, Zina. She's sick and asked me to help with her children."

"When are you planning to be home? What time?" I asked. I was feeling suddenly frightened.

"I really don't know. However long it will take." Mother paused and then added. "I made a pot of soup last night. Natasha gave me half a chicken, so have some for dinner. Don't wait for us.

Before going to school I opened my window a slight, unnoticeable crack, so I could slip quietly into my room without using the front or back entrance. I was so nervous at school I couldn't concentrate and could hardly practice at the music school. It was already past three o'clock. Time to go home. I walked slowly—it was too hot and humid. In the west, ominous dark clouds were forming.

"Thunder storm coming," I murmured. I took the back road. Sneaking quietly through the bushes, I opened the window. *No sound, no sound, Lara.* In a couple of seconds I was in my room, and locked the window extra tightly.

Holding my breath, I tiptoed to the wall separating me from the NKVD man's room and listened for a while. Complete silence. *Good, he's not home.* I breathed easier.

Worrisome thoughts churned in my mind. *I wonder if Natasha is home?* I felt hungry. There was the soup in the kitchen. But no, no way was I going to leave my room. I lay down on the couch. Slowly my eyes closed.

Suddenly, a loud knock on the door made me jump. I put my hand over my mouth. My heart was beating rapidly. Another knock. I looked at the window. *Should I run?* Then Natasha's voice rang out pleasantly, "Is anybody home?"

"Natasha," I sighed in relief. "Just a moment, just a moment," I called out. My hand was shaking when I unlocked the door.

Natasha looked at me. "What's wrong?"

"Nothing. I fell asleep. I'm glad you woke me up. Please come in."

Natasha's face was all smiles. In her hands she held a roll of multicolored fabric. Extending it to me she said, "See, see how beautiful? Look at these colors, Lara, and here, touch. Doesn't it feel like silk?" With a short laugh she added, "Not that I know how silk feels, but what do you think?"

I stroked the fabric a couple of times. "Oh, yes, it is really lovely, and, well, maybe it is silk." I smiled at her. "Where did you get it?" I asked.

Natasha was jubilant. "I exchanged it for two pieces of bacon—big pieces—Boris brought me last time from the country. Now Boris is out in the fields again, but he'll be back in four days." She put the roll of fabric on the table and stroked it lovingly.

"Lara, dear, I am going to the seamstress right now, but I don't have matching thread. Maybe your mother has some." She looked pleadingly into my eyes. I patted her on the shoulder.

"We'll find something."

I went into my parent's bedroom and brought out the sewing basket. Natasha looked in. "I never saw so many spools of thread," she exclaimed.

It took her quite a long time to select one. "Yes, I think this will match the best," she finally said.

Through the open door Natasha saw the full-length mirror in the next room. "Can I look at it in the mirror?" She asked, "I just want to see how I look in these colors."

"Of course, you can." It was really fun for me to see her so excited. Putting the thread on the table, she went to the mirror and draped herself in the fabric. I followed her with the basket. She turned from side to side, smiling at her reflection in the mirror.

"Oh, Lara, I am so happy! I've never had anything so wonderful in my life, and I look good in these colors," she said approvingly. I want the dress to be ready in three days." With shining eyes, she added, "I want to wear it when Boris gets home." She kissed me on the cheek and left.

I shook my head. *How little was needed to bring so much happiness.*

"Now, now, Lara, you are getting philosophical," I chided myself sighing. *"Better put the sewing basket away and lock the door."*

Coming back to my room, I noticed the thread Natasha selected on the table. "What a silly woman, she forgot it." I picked up the thread, went to the hall and knocked on Natasha's door. I tried the handle; the door was locked. *Well, I might still catch her outside,* I thought and ran through the hall to the front door, but I did not have the chance to open it. A strong hand grabbed me and pulled me back. I heard the NKVD man's mocking voice.

"Natasha is gone. It's just you and me, and I'm tired of your stubbornness." I felt myself being picked up and carried into his room. Shock immobilized me, but when he pushed me on his bed, I screamed.

"You can scream all you want. Nobody's home. Better behave," he motioned to close the door to his room. It took me a second to jump from the bed and run to the open window. I was already on the windowsill, but he grabbed me and pushed me back on the bed again. I was surprised at his strength.

"So, you want to play cat and mouse." There was anger in his voice . "All right, we'll play cat and mouse."

Like a big spider, he hovered over me. I looked at him with horror.

"Let me go, oh, please, let me go," my voice trembled.

Suddenly, he grabbed the braid on the back of my head and pulled my head down, with the weight of his body pinning me to the bed. I smelled his acrid tobacco odor close to me face.

Fight, Lara, fight! Was my only thought. I tried to push him back, turning my head from right to left to avoid his lips, but they covered mine again and again. I felt suffocated.

He was getting wilder.

In a moment he grabbed my arm forcefully.

"Let go, you bully." I was fighting, twisting, hitting him with my fists. I shouted, "No, no… no." Grabbing his hair with my fingers, I tried to push his face away from me.

He hissed with pain, and I saw an angry, red-flushed face above me.

"You little devil. You want it rough, you'll get it rough," he said through clenched teeth. His right hand formed a fist, and I closed my eyes, expecting a blow.

"Don't do that, don't hit her, leave her alone!" The hysterical voice of Natasha rang in my ears. I opened my eyes. She was standing in the doorway. I realized that he did not have a chance to close it. Startled, he turned around. He let go of my braid and relaxed his grip on me.

Using all the strength I had left, I freed myself, lurching awkwardly for the door. Pushing Natasha aside, I rushed through the hall to the bathroom, locking the door behind me. I placed my back firmly against it, just in case. Breathing in gulps of air, I felt my heart racing. The words repeated again and again in my brain, *"Oh my God, oh, my God."*

I noticed my ripped blouse. Somehow I wrapped it around and tucked it into my skirt. *Now wash, wash.* For a long time I splashed cold water on my face, rinsed my mouth several times, trying to scrub the slimy feeling off my lips. With shaking hands, I undid my braid, combed my hair and braided it again. Not daring to look at my face in the mirror, I closed my eyes and leaned on the door. *What now, what now?* I listened for a while. Everything was quiet. Finally, I opened the door just a crack—the hall was empty. Slipping quietly into my room, I turned the key.

Now change the blouse. I'm never going to wear it again. I tucked the blouse safely under the mattress. *I'll dispose of it tomorrow.* Suddenly I shivered. *What if Natasha had not come back?* But she had. She had and I was safe.. Natasha saved me. *Oh, dear God, how can I thank her? I am in debt to her for the rest of my life.* I stood in the middle of the room, jittery and nervous. *I have to go and see Natasha. I have to talk to her. But if that man . . . No, no, he wouldn't do anything now, not after Natasha stopped him.* No, that's over.

Without hesitation, I went out to the hall and knocked on Natasha's door. No answer. I tried the handle and the door opened. Natasha was standing by the window looking out. "Natasha, I came to thank you for saving my life," I said and heard the shake in my voice again.

She turned and looked at me for a while, then said, "Saved your life? What big words. Oh, how naive you can be, Lara. The truth is I ruined your life and the life of your parents." She shook her head and added, "And worst of all, I ruined my own life, too."

I stood speechless in the doorway. *What was she saying? What did she mean?* I had never seen her face like that. I could say it was tragic.

She started to pace the room, wringing her hands. "I am stupid, stupid. I should've known better. How did I dare stop him? Why did I have to come back?"

I noticed the roll of fabric on the bed and thread on the floor. I probably dropped the thread in the hall when the NKVD man assaulted me.

She kicked the thread, "Stupid, stupid thread."

Natasha was getting more and more agitated. Suddenly she stopped in front of me. "And you, why did you have to fight him? Your life is not worth anything now. Do you know how angry he is, and at me, too?"

She turned around and started walking, again talking. "For once in my life I have it good. Boris likes his job, so much food, we're never hungry, and all the things I have now—so many clothes." She picked up the fabric from the bed and threw it on the floor. "If not for this stupid dress," she almost choked, then faced me again. "Do you understand that for the first time in my life we have two rooms, two whole rooms to ourselves? For years, Boris and I lived in just a corner of a room..."

"But why should you be afraid? What can he do to you?" I interrupted her finally.

Furiously, Natasha looked at me. "I *stopped* him. I dared to interrupt him. He told me before he left that I'll pay for that... and what can he *do*? He works for the NKVD. You must know how the almighty NKVD..." She paused, took a gulp of breath and continued. "He can arrest Boris and me, and send us to a labor camp, even shoot us."

"So why did you stop him?" I almost shouted.

She shook her head a couple of times and said more calmly. "When I came back for the thread I forgot, the door to his room was open. I heard your screams. I couldn't help myself. I couldn't let him do this to you." Again she shook her head. "You remind me of my sister. It was as if she were being attacked."

Exhausted she sat on her bed and bent her head down. For a while there was silence in the room.

Then she looked at me. "Lara, come here and sit beside me."

Automatically I did what she asked.

She turned her flushed face to me. "Lara, listen — listen good. You must understand that the only chance you have is for you to go to him willingly, tonight, after he comes home. Tell him you got your senses back, and ask his forgiveness."

I stirred, but she grabbed my hand and looked pleadingly into my eyes. "Don't you understand girl, that this is the only way to save yourself and your parents? He can send all three of you to jail, or labor camps. And do you know how long you would last? You will become a personal servant with absolutely no rights. No rights!"

I listened with horror. Her face was close to mine. She almost whispered into my ear. "You have no choice, Lara, dear. I know it's terrible for you, but this way, after he is satisfied, he'll leave you alone. His wife'll come soon."

She grabbed my shoulders and shook me. "Just listen, girl, listen."

I looked at her, not really comprehending what she was asking of me.

"Natasha. What are you saying? Do you understand what you want from me? How can you?"

Suddenly she pushed me away and got up. "No, really, why am I even talking to you? Stupid, stupid girl." Turning to me, hands on her hips, she suddenly shouted. "Look at her, just look at her. Her body is so precious. I saved her life — ha, ha, ha. You know what? Your body is not worth a kopeck. I wonder how you'll feel when the NKVD soldiers come to arrest your father and mother?" Looking exhausted, she pointed to the door. "Now get out. I have to think how to save my own skin."

She sat on the bed, covered her face with her hands, and started crying loudly and desperately.

Quietly I left the room. My thoughts were in complete turmoil.

17 DECISION TO MAKE

Back in my room I paced the floor back and forward from wall to door. "What am I going to do?" I asked myself. Natasha's suggestion made me sick to my stomach. Tormenting thoughts swirled through my mind.

Of my own free will, go to this man? Oh, my God, but if I don't, is he really so powerful that he can arrest us?

Knowing the system, I knew he could. It was enough to say he overheard us talking against Stalin. Many people were punished with life for less. Mother and father dragged to prison, interrogated, maybe tortured! The familiar feeling of physical pain shot through my body. Oh, no, no, no! Pacing the room, I caught the reflection of my face in the mirror above my piano. Wild, red eyes, flushed face. I looked terrible. One look at me and my parents would ask questions, and I could not tell them anything. *Compose yourself, compose yourself,* I whispered, but my head felt as if it were cracking.

With both hands I squeezed my temples. If only I could rest for a while and not think of anything.

Quickly I made my bed, undressed, put on my nightgown and slid between the sheets. *Yes, that's better. Now relax. Oh, how tired I am, how tired.* I closed my eyes, trying to block my thoughts. Exhausted, I must have dozed.

A cool hand on my forehead brought me back to reality. I opened my eyes. Mother's worried face was above me. "Are you all right?" She asked softly. "You didn't touch the food I left you."

I looked at her dear face. "I don't feel well," I said in a trembling voice. She sat on the edge of my bed, and I saw fear in her eyes.

"Anything hurt?"

"No," I shook my head.

She touched my forehead again. "I don't think you have a fever."

I sat up and embraced her fiercely.

"Oh, mama, just hold me, just hold me." An overwhelming desire to cry engulfed me. We held each other tightly. Mother gently stroked my hair.

"My poor girl, my poor girl. If only I could help you, if I only knew how. My God, this life is so terrible." I heard tears in her voice. She sighed and added, "I know you miss Tonia very much."

I clenched my teeth, took a big breath and said, "Yes, yes, I miss Tonia so much, but don't worry, it's just a moment of weakness." I pulled back and looking into her eyes, continued. "See, I am already smiling, so please smile back, all right?"

She shook her head and said, "I'm so worried about you."

Father came into the room. "Nata, I heated the soup. We have to eat something." Looking at me he added, "Lara, get up, put on your robe, and set the table."

I busied myself with the chores, even ate a little bit. By 10 o'clock, my parents retired to their bedroom.

Again I was faced with decision-making. Should I submit myself to this horrible man? Right before the war I read Dostoyevsky's novel, *Crime and Punishment*. It made a deep impression on me. Sonia, the heroine, an innocent girl of seventeen, makes a decision to sell her body for money. Her father is an unemployed drunkard; her stepmother has two small children. There is no food, no heat in their meager lodging. Sonia goes on the street and sells her body to save her family. *How noble,* I thought then, when I was reading the book.

I crawled back to bed and covered my head with the blanket. "You have no choice," I told myself, remembering the events in the man's room—his hands on my body, his slimy lips on my mouth, the tobacco stench. *I can't do it, I can't. Oh, dear, almighty God, please help me,* I prayed; yet I wanted to shout, to beat the wall with my fists, to howl like a dog. *I'd rather die, I'd rather die.* I sat up in bed. Yes, death was the solution. All three of us should die. All I had to do was go to my parents and tell them everything. They would agree. It was useless to live this kind of life. Yes, we would refuse to live under

Stalin's cruel system. I did not want to be violated; my parents would not want me to be violated. They would understand. Mother had sleeping pills. We could take them and fall asleep. No pain, no decisions to make, yes, no torments. I lay back and closed my eyes. Yes, peace and quiet. I breathed deeply. Then my thoughts turned to other directions. *So, you want to kill your parents, too, Lara! Bravo, bravo, that's really noble. You don't want to sacrifice yourself, oh, no, not you. There's a war going on — thousands are suffering and dying, and you think only of yourself. You back out before any hardship.*

Hardship? This is more than a hardship. It is not only a violation of my body, but a violation of my soul, my spirit, everything that is clean and noble in me. My inner self.

I felt all twisted inside. I wanted to cry long and loud, like Natasha. Instead I pushed a corner of my pillow in my mouth and tried to control myself.

There was a sound in the NKVD man's room. I listened for a moment. Yes, he had returned. Slowly I got up and put on my robe. I went over to the separating wall. I could hear him moving about his room. There was a loud noise as if something had fallen, a chair maybe? After a while, I heard a bed creak, then silence.

It is time, it is time, I have to go to him, I thought, but still I lingered by the wall. I was about to move when I heard voices. What was this? I put my ear to the wall again. Definitely a woman's voice. Natasha's voice. Now a man's voice — angry — and Natasha's pleading. Too bad I could not distinguish the words; my heart was beating so loudly in my chest.

Natasha probably came to ask his forgiveness. Yes, that must be it.

Now the voices calmed down, then came the thumping of a bed, loud thumping. *What was going on in there? Was he attacking Natasha?* I jumped away from the wall as from a hot plate. I understood now, Natasha came to him of her own free will. I remembered her words, "I have to think of something to save me and Boris." Suddenly I felt so weak. Tension released, I was drained.

I crawled into bed and buried my head in the pillows, trying to block out the noise in the next room. Gradually a numbness overcame my mind and strangely, my body felt at peace. I fell into a deep, sound sleep.

18   FACING REALITY

The sound of voices wakened me. *No, please, I still want to sleep, I want to sleep,* but the voices would not go away, mother's and Vasia's. I opened my eyes. Mama was standing by the open door to the hall. Vasia was probably in the hall. I heard his voice,

"But she can't sleep all day. It's already afternoon."

"Please, Vasia, not so loud," mother's voice was muted. "She wasn't feeling well yesterday. I'm really worried about her. I have to let her sleep as long as she can."

"All right, Aunt Nata, but tell her Misha is back in town from college, and he is coming to see me tonight. Maybe we'll play cards or something."

"Yes, Vasia, I'll tell her." Mother closed the door quietly. I pretended to be asleep, but the events of yesterday were coming to my mind. Natasha, Natasha! She came to him to offer herself instead of me. She must have been sure I would not go to this man.

"I have to think of a way to save my life." Those were her words. Survival, no matter what. How terrible, and how disgusting.

But weren't you ready to sacrifice yourself, Lara? Again, the big word, sacrifice. *And would you have really done it? Why did you stay at that wall so long?* I felt fear and panic. *What is going to happen to us now? Will the NKVD man take revenge? Nothing I can change, I thought.* Slowly the feeling of resignation came over me. I had to get up and face daily life. Vasia wanted something. Oh, yes, he said Misha was in town.

I remembered the New Year's Eve concert, Misha's kind, blue eyes, his lips against my skin. For the first time in my life, a boy kissed my hand. But that was another lifetime.

I could not see Misha. I could not face him, not after what happened yesterday. I was safe, but I was not the same person anymore. I felt blemished. The rest of the day I stayed in my room. I told my mother I had a lot of homework, many tests to prepare for, and it was the truth.

In the evening Vasia burst into the room. "What's wrong with you, sleeping all day? Misha wants to come over. I think he is dying to see you," he said, winking at me.

I looked at Vasia calmly. "I can't, not now, not later. I'll be busy all next week, you know, the end of the school year."

"You can spare an hour."

"No, I have many assignments, and I have to prepare for a recital next Sunday, so leave me alone, please."

"You won't change your mind?"

"No, I really can't."

Vasia looked at me thoughtfully. "You know, you seem rather strange today, but, as you wish." He left muttering something under his breath.

For two nights I could hear voices, the creaking of a bed. Then Natasha's husband came home. Poor woman, how could she face him? I saw her a couple of times in the kitchen — her eyes were red. We were avoiding each other. I plunged into studying and practicing, anything to keep from thinking. Nothing I can do now, I told myself. Whatever has to be, will be. Days went by, one after another. Grisha came up to me a couple of times at school wanting to talk, but I brushed him off.

Saturday brought the last day of school. Sunday, would be my first, and possibly last, piano recital. *So, do the best you can do, Lara, the best you can do.* My recital consisted of a Bach invention, a Mozart sonata, two Chopin nocturnes, and a Mendelssohn concerto.

The music school was packed. A couple of students performed before me. I was last. That made me more jittery. Finally, my turn came. As soon as I touched the keys a strange sensation took over. I felt suddenly free. My fingers on the delicate white keys gave me a freedom to express my innermost feelings. Through this music I could complain, be angry, pour out my despair, even curse and cry with my fingers. It felt good, playing. I was almost happy.

Last chords—it was over.

Applause. Loud applause.

I was in a daze. Backstage my teacher came to me and gave me a big hug. "Lara, dear girl, your playing was beautiful and exciting. You really surprised me with the maturity of your performance. I'm proud of you."

I saw mother and father's smiling faces. People I didn't know were approaching and congratulating me. "Well, well, well," I heard Vasia's mocking voice, "the star is born." He handed me the program and added, "My lady, may I have your autograph, please?"

Then I saw a tall figure, Misha making his way towards me. He held out a little bouquet of flowers. "I enjoyed your playing immensely," he smiled eagerly.

I smiled back at him, at everybody. For the first time since the beginning of this nightmare I felt a warm feeling of accomplishment and satisfaction.

19   REVENGE

T he next afternoon I took father for a walk. Again we talked about Russia. "It is such a vast country, vast and sad. The people have been oppressed so many times," he said. "Tartars, Swedes, French, Germans, and now worst of all, communism, but their hearts are strong, and I believe they will survive again. I'm sure of that. Only I'm not going to live long enough to see it," he added in a resigned, somber tone.

Neither will I, I thought.

When we came home we found mother pale and shaking with a slip of paper in her hand.

"A soldier brought this just ten minutes ago," she said. "We have to report to the NKVD headquarters at six o'clock this evening."

Father grabbed the paper. I came close to see what was written on it. It stated that my father and mother had to appear with their passports at the NKVD offices.

So it is happening, here is his revenge. My parents will be arrested. The thought shot through my mind.

"It's all my fault, all my fault," I said suddenly. The pain was so great I could not control myself. I knelt on the floor and broke down, sobbing.

"Mama, papa, please forgive me. It is because of me, but really, I would've done it. I was ready to go, but you see, Natasha…" Tears were choking me. My parents looked at me, startled. Mother knelt beside me.

"Child, child, what are you talking about? What is your fault?" She put her arms around me, trying to help me up. "Lara, calm down. Get up, darling. Let's go sit on the couch. We'll talk."

But now I could not stop crying. "Mama, mama, you have to understand, if not for Natasha I would have been the one, but she took my place. I was saved. Oh, God, please forgive me."

I went into hysterics. They picked me up and put me on the couch. "Let her cry," father said. Both of them sat next to me. Mama was stroking my back.

"Shhh, child, shhh." Slowly I calmed down. There were no emotions left in me, just pain.

"I'll go and talk to Maria. Vasia's mother will help." Mother was thinking out loud.

After a while they both came back. Aunt Maria sat next to me. "Lara, come to my house. I will take care of you."

"No." I jumped from the couch. "No, I will go to the NKVD with my parents," I almost shouted. "Whatever they do to them, they will have to do to me. I can't let them go without me."

"Lara, no," my parents said in unison.

"Oh, don't you see, I must go with you. I must. It's the only way," I mumbled.

Something must have shown in my face because father said, "Let her go with us."

I washed my face and combed my hair. I was not of age to have a passport, so I took my student identification card. We walked to the NKVD offices in silence. It was a big, gray building. At the entrance father presented the summoning paper and a soldier led us through a long corridor to an empty room with simply some chairs and benches.

"Wait here," he said gruffly. After a while the door to the next room opened, and a man in the NKVD uniform summoned us in. There was a big desk in the middle of the room with lots of papers on it. Two windows let in the setting sun. Even though there was no warmth in it the room felt hot and stuffy.

The man sat behind the desk looking at some papers. He was short and skinny with pale, unhealthy skin and dark hair. All three of us were standing in front of the desk. There were some chairs, but he did not ask us to sit down. I remembered Grisha's words. *Some wait in silence like obedient cattle.*

Finally, he looked up and said, "You are declared an enemy of the State. This falls under the 11th paragraph of our law, which means you are not allowed to dwell in places exceeding a population of five thousand. Therefore, in a maximum of seven days you must leave town. If you disobey, you will be arrested. Now, your passports."

Without a word, my parents handed him their passports.

We have to leave town, I thought, *only leave town, that's all. Oh, dear, almighty God, we are free to go, all three of us.* Tears started streaming from my eyes, tears of great relief.

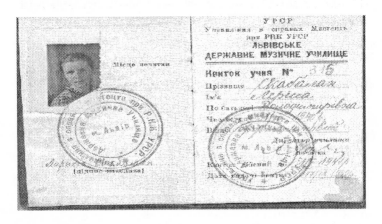

Put the 11ᵗʰ paragraph here, too.

The man pointed at me. "Daughter?" He asked. Father nodded.

I pulled out my student card and said, "Put the 11ᵗʰ paragraph here, too."

He looked at the card and returned it to me. "I can put the paragraph only on passports. When you are eighteen and issued one, then it will be added." He started writing and stamping the passports. After a few moments he gave them back to my parents.

Without a word, we left the room. We walked fast, trying to put distance between us and the NKVD offices. Mama and papa talked in low voices.

On my mind there was only one thought—leave town, leave town. Tomorrow will not be too soon. I really could not comprehend that this was the only revenge, but it was rather a blessing. I felt almost joy, after I expected the worst. They labeled us *enemies of the state*. What did we do wrong? Anyway, it would be better to live in a small community and not be visible; maybe then they would leave us alone. "They" signified for me, Stalin and his cohorts. "They" were the true enemies of the State, the country and the people of the whole world.

Mama tugged at my sleeve. "Lara, we have to talk, and better here in the open air than at home." By now we were walking by the city park. We sat on an unoccupied bench away from the crowds.

"All right," father said. "Your mother and I have decided to try to find a room in Willanovo. It's a small community about ten kilometers from town. My former client and his wife have retired there."

"The one with the strawberry farm?" I interrupted.

"Yes, yes, Lara, and tomorrow I will visit them and see if they can accommodate us. You and mother have to start packing."

"We will move as soon as we can, yes?" I pleaded.

"As soon as we can," mother sighed. Then, looking straight into my eyes, she said, "Lara, what were you talking about before we went to the NKVD? What was your fault? What's this talk about Natasha?"

I shook my head. "Mama, dearest, someday I will be able to tell you, but not now. I can't now. I was so scared, so scared." My lips started to tremble.

She put her fingers on my lips. "Shhh, child, shhh. You will tell me when you are ready. Now let's go home. We have been through enough today."

20   THE MOVE

The following days passed quickly. Father was able to rent the front room from his friends in the next town. Their property was not yet nationalized. The Soviet authorities were so busy in town that small communities were still untouched.

Our living quarters were shrinking. From two rooms we were now moving into one. We had to limit ourselves to bare necessities. My parent's big bed, my couch, a dining room table, chairs, mother's big dresser with the mirror, and finally, my piano. Whatever we did not need was moved to Aunt Marie and Vasia's house. Father rented a transport platform with two strong horses. It took several trips to transport everything. We had lots of help; Vasia, Misha, even ever-gloomy Grisha came to give us a hand.

Misha and Grisha took an instant dislike to each other and it was unbelievably funny to listen to them bicker constantly about completely unimportant things. For instance, how to best tie the rope around transported furniture, or how to place the piano on the platform, and so on. Vasia, of course, was teasing them all the time, which made matters even worse.

During these days I never saw the NKVD man. Natasha told us he left to bring his family. Now we understood why we had to vacate our two rooms. He needed extra space. It was a simple matter to add an 11th paragraph to our passports and push us out of the house.

Finally, everything was moved. It was time for us to leave. I went for the last time to our two empty rooms and looked around. Part of my life lay in these two rooms, in the whole house, the house of my childhood, such a happy childhood. In my early life I was sheltered, pampered, and probably spoiled. Life was presented to me in rosy colors. I realized that was why the events of the last ten months were so hard on me. All that I went through lately should help my spirit grow and make me stronger, help me face whatever was in store for me. *Who am I*, I asked myself. *Why should I want something special for me?* Reality was hard and cruel, but maybe there was a reason for everything, and I needed to not be the one to complain and judge.

Natasha was waiting for me in the hall. She looked at me but couldn't hide the embarrassment in her eyes. I came close and embraced her. "Don't think badly of me," she said so softly I could barely make it out.

"Oh, Natasha, how could I?" I pulled myself from her. "I understand, I do." Pausing a little, I added. "You know, I was about to go to him myself."

Suddenly, without thinking, I picked up her hand, kissed it, and left abruptly. A little voice in the back of my head said, *You are getting too melodramatic now.*

21 IN THE COUNTRY

It was the beginning of July. The days were hot and full of sunshine. The house we moved into was charming. It consisted of two bedrooms, a kitchen, and a spacious front room with big windows. It was light and airy. The French doors opened onto a large veranda, four steps led to a garden full of flowers, shrubs and several fruit trees.

Behind the house was a strawberry plantation and a vegetable garden. We settled in the front room and arranged our furniture. The kitchen had to be shared with our landlords. They were a lovely couple in their sixties—Andrei Ivanovich and Olga Petrovana. Andrei Ivanovich was a tall, gaunt individual with a bald head and dark, busy eyebrows. He had a kind smile and welcomed us openheartedly.

He was especially glad to see my piano.

"How wonderful," he exclaimed. "That's what I miss, a piano. Last year we gave ours to our daughter when she got married, and I haven't played since."

"Please, you can use mine any time you wish," I said.

He became enthusiastic. "We can play four hands. I have a lot of music, and you know," he winked at me, "I can sing, too." He seemed to be such a nice old man.

His wife, Olga Petrovana, was short and the best expression to describe her would have to be "round". Gray hair piled on top of her head, rosy cheeks, blue eyes and a snub nose completed the picture.

"How pleasant to have a young creature again in our house," she said when she saw me. "A little pale and thin, poor child," she stroked my cheek, "but don't you worry, with good food and fresh air, you will improve in no time." And really, with every day I felt better and calmer. Like after a deadly sickness, I was coming back to life.

I would get up early in the morning and quietly sneak outside. It was such a pleasure to walk in the garden so early in the day, breathing fresh, enticing air and being surrounded by the beauty of nature. After breakfast I would help our landlords with their daily chores. I worked in the garden weeding and picking strawberries. Every day so many baskets had to be delivered to the stores. In the afternoons, mother and I walked in the woods that surrounded our small community. There we gathered some of the mushrooms that had started to appear.

Best of all, I liked the evenings. After dinner we assembled on the veranda for tea. Olga Petrovana always had some baked goodies, and we would talk freely, but still with hushed voices. As we talked,

Andrei Ivanovich would sit at the piano and play. Sometimes he entertained us in his soft baritone, with old Russian folk songs and gypsy romances. It was as if we had been transported to a different world.

22   NEW LIFE

In the whole community, consisting of approximately fifty households, there was only one general store that supplied milk, bread, potatoes, and very few other items. Occasionally, different items were available, and the news would spread and everybody would rush to the store and stand in line. Somehow, Olga Petrovana was always one of the first to get the information, and then excitedly she would shout, "Quick, quick, everybody to the store. They are giving out sugar—one pound per person!"

I enjoyed every day that went by, so the weeks passed rapidly. One Sunday around noon, I was picking strawberries and putting them into the baskets to be delivered to the store early Monday morning. It was hot. The sun's rays were streaming on me mercilessly. "I should go and get my sun hat," I thought, but was too lazy to get up from the ground. I ate some strawberries, selecting the biggest and juiciest. They tasted so good. A couple more baskets and I would be done picking. I hurried, perspiration ran from my forehead, and I wiped it with my hands.

"Hello, Lara." I heard the voice and turned around. It was Misha, about 100 yards away and approaching slowly. All the blood rushed to my head. I jumped from the ground.

Oh, my God, I look terrible, my mind was racing. I was wearing an old, faded dress, stained throughout with strawberry juice. My legs were indescribably dirty, bare; hands, oh, hands were the worst; hair in disarray. I stood in front of Misha extremely embarrassed.

"Don't look at me," I said, "I am a mess."

"Mess or not, you look much better than you did before, rosy cheeks, sunburned nose." He started laughing, "And all this war paint on your face is very becoming."

I looked at him, "War paint?" And then I remembered. I wiped perspiration from my face with dirty, stained hands. I became even more embarrassed. Misha stopped laughing.

"Don't worry," he said, "you look great." Pointing to the empty baskets, he asked, "Need help?"

Together we filled the baskets in a short time and then carried the strawberries to the house. I went to wash. Looking in the mirror I started laughing at myself—dirty smudges on my forehead, strawberry stains around my mouth and on my nose.

It was a lovely afternoon. We played a game of croquet, then Olga Petrovana asked us to pick some cherries from her tree, and we all made *vareniki*—a

Ukrainian dish, with dumplings stuffed with sour cherries. Misha stayed for dinner, then in the evening, as usual, we had tea on the veranda. It was just like the good old times, the ghost of Stalin faded for the day.

It was time for Misha to catch the train back to town. I accompanied him to the railroad station. We walked by ripening grain fields. The evening was full of odd, slightly random scents. It felt as if nature was resting after the day's heat, waiting for the coolness of the night.

Misha told me he got a job for the summer and asked if he could visit us again. "It is so peaceful here, like another world," he said.

"You know, I thought about that, too," I replied. "We don't even listen to the Soviet radio and don't read the newspapers. Here is the first time in a very long time that life feels remotely normal again. Of course, you can come any time. We'll be happy to see you."

"How about next Sunday?" He smiled.

"Sure." I smiled back.

At the station I said good-bye to Misha and slowly walked home. The sun was setting behind the crowns of the trees. I thought about Misha. I felt comfortable with him. He could be a good friend, so calm, reliable, clumsy and funny sometimes, and, oh, we laughed today. The horrors of last month were someplace far away.

That night there was a thunderstorm. Nature was demonstrating its anger. Lightening flashes came one after another, and thunder roared. I was never afraid of thunderstorms. I liked the turbulence in the sky, the release of tension.

Morning came bright and shiny. The strawberry season was over; it was time to pick cherries. As with the strawberries, our landlord had to supply quotas established by the authorities. Andrei Ivanovich was fuming. "Some Soviet officials came, counted my trees, and told me how many pounds I have to deliver. They didn't even ask what is my usual crop. Luckily, I have good cherries this year, so maybe we'll have some left over for ourselves, but what if next year we have a poor crop?" So when we started to pick, Olga told me to fill up the baskets with any kind of cherries.

"Even rotten?" I asked.

"Yes, rotten, dried out, wormy, who cares?" She replied angrily. "If we give them the best, I won't have anything for myself."

I felt uneasy.

"Look, Lara, we delivered to the warehouses the best strawberries. You know, because you picked them yourself. And did you see what kind of berries were sold in the store? Half rotten; because it took many days for those bureaucrats to finally distribute them to the people. Before the occupation we always sold our product privately so the customers got everything fresh."

"I can't argue with that," I said, "but..."

She interrupted me. "The system is beating us, so we have to learn how to beat the system."

I did not say anything, but her reasoning gave me something to think about. Were our own moral values changing? Was this a necessity for survival? Still, it was very unpleasant for me to fill the baskets with bad berries.

Andrei Ivanovich was laughing. "Poor girl, I guess Olga Petrovana is corrupting you. I don't like the idea myself, but then I would be without my favorite preserves in the winter."

"All right," I answered, "we are condemning communists for what they are doing, and then we turn around and do immoral things ourselves."

"Us, immoral? Look, Lara, I worked hard all my life, saved some money, bought this place, dreamed to retire pleasantly. Now if I fulfill honestly their unreasonable quotas, I won't have anything for myself."

I wanted to say something, but he stopped me. "Wait, wait, let me finish. I just wanted to say that, yes, I'm paid for delivering fruit, but that is so little, and anyway, I can hardly buy anything with the money. So what is there for me? And for the land to produce, I have to work hard, fertilize, trim, weed, plant, transplant." Andrei Ivanovich was getting more and more excited. "Listen, listen, this year Soviets let me have this place, but next year I'm sure it will be nationalized. And then you know what?" He looked at me and I saw anger in his face. "The Soviets will probably let me stay in the place and pay me monthly wages." He raised his voice. "But do you think I will work as hard as I worked for myself? Never, never. This place is mine." He choked, and I saw that he was embarrassed.

There was a silence, and then he continued, sadly pointing to the garden. "Everything will rot, like the whole Soviet economy is already rotting. I hope one day the Communists realize what monstrous injustices they are doing to the people."

I had nothing to say to the poor man.

23   A LETTER FROM TONIA

O n Saturday, when I came back from the woods where mother and I had been picking mushrooms, I found Grisha on the veranda. Without a word, he handed me a letter. I recognized Tonia's handwriting. With trembling hands I opened it. It was sent from kazakstan, a republic in the Soviet Union. The letter was short.

> *We survived. Now we are on the steppes of Kazakstan. We had to dig our own earth homes. All the people we came with helped each other. I'm working on a farm, cultivating the land. Mama has to work, too. Lara, please send us some warm clothing and some tea—we can exchange it for food with the local people. Andrei is so thin. Please pray for us. I embrace you and kiss you.*
>
> *Tonia*

I handed the letter to Grisha. While he was reading, I looked at him. I had not seen Grisha for the last couple of weeks, and he seemed to be thinner. Something indescribably sad was in his face. He finished reading and sighed. "Thank God they survived the horrific conditions on that train, but earth houses? How will they live in those in winter? In Kazakstan the cold can be extremely severe."

I remembered that after Tonia's deportation, Grisha took care of all their belongings, transporting them to his aunt's house.

"You have all of Tonia's things?" I asked.

"Yes, and you have to come and decide what clothing we should send and, of course, the tea. We have to get as much as we can."

We agreed that at the latest by next Wednesday, we should mail the package. The following days I was busy collecting tea. Even Olga Petrovana brought out all she had. I was embarrassed to accept it.

"How about evening tea?" I asked.

"Dear girl, do you think I could take a sip of tea knowing that your friend needs it? Don't worry, Lara, from now on we will drink chamomile tea. Plenty of chamomile flowers growing around here." She smiled and winked at me. "It will be your job to collect the flowers, and I will dry them."

Misha came again on Sunday and he, too, offered to hunt for tea and helped me to gather chamomile flowers. In a couple of days we were ready to send the package. I hated going to town, but I had to help getting everything together. Grisha found out that we could send one package every three months. It was comforting that we could be of help. Tonia was now constantly on my mind, and I felt guilty living in this quiet community and not being forced to work as hard as she did.

On Wednesday I took the train to town. Although I was born there and had loved it, the town now felt hostile to me. Red banners with the hammer and sickle were everywhere. Stalin's statue appeared in squares, and, of course, his portrait was in every store window. From the station I walked quickly to Grisha's house. Vasia was there, too. He brought one package of tea. "That is all I had in the house," he said.

Red banners with the hammer and sickle were everywhere.

It took us quite a long time to put together everything that we thought was most essential. In three months we could send another package. Grisha was so sad. I tried unsuccessfully to hold my tears. Even Vasia was very serious.

"What's happening at our house?" I asked him.

"Now that the NKVD man's wife and daughter are there, I don't think Natasha and her husband will remain much longer."

I looked at Vasia with the question in my eyes. "Why not?"

"Natasha told my mother that his wife constantly argues with her."

I shrugged my shoulders and murmured, "Well, that is their own business."

Finally everything was neatly arranged. Vasia and Grisha bound it strongly together and labeled it according to Tonia's instructions. Then I sat down and wrote Tonia a letter. Quickly, I told her about my life and asked God's blessing upon her and her family. Grisha and Vasia added a few sentences.

"Want to come with us to the post office, Lara?" Grisha asked.

I thought for a moment and said, "No, I better catch the train home." I wanted to get out of town as soon as possible, but Grisha's aunt insisted that I stay and have a bite to eat.

"Can you keep me company for awhile?" She asked. "I need to talk to you." Today was the first day that I met Grisha's aunt. She was in her seventies perhaps, quite frail, but immaculately dressed and groomed, short in stature, with gray hair in a bun at the back of her head. She resembled the old portraits of the last century. Her house consisted of three small rooms and a kitchen.

Grisha occupied one room, she the other, and one room served as a living and dining area.

With my help we prepared two sandwiches, then sat down at the table. The old lady smiled. "I can't offer you tea. Grisha confiscated all I had, so milk must do." For a while we ate in silence.

Finally she said, "I am so worried about Grisha. Something is going on. He seems excessively preoccupied. He often goes to see friends, so he says. Sometimes several young men come here, always through the back door and they lock themselves in Grisha's room for hours."

"Did you talk to Grisha about it?" I asked.

"Oh, I did, several times, but he just shrugs his shoulders and tells me not to worry. But I do worry, he is all I've got." She sighed. "Lara, can you find out what is going on? Or maybe you know already?"

I felt uneasy. The thought went through my mind, *Is Grisha really organizing an underground?* But I could not tell the poor woman about my suspicions. I simply said, "I can try to find out what those meetings are about, but I doubt that Grisha will confide in me. I see him very seldom now."

Hope was in her voice when she said, "When he visits you in the country, please talk to him, and tell him not to do anything foolish." Tears filled Grisha's aunt's eyes. I promised to do whatever I could and tried to calm her. On my way home I had much to think about.

I was almost positive that some kind of organization was being created, but my God, it was extremely dangerous—dangerous and yet, exciting. At least Grisha was doing something. I admired him for that. Subconsciously I knew that successful resistance against Stalin was impossible. Sooner or later the NKVD would find out about the conspiracy and crush it. Still, suffering, even death, might be worth it for the good of the cause, fighting and resisting to the end. Surely it was better than submission and passivity. For the next couple of days I was very quiet.

I could not sleep well. Every night I stayed in the garden or sat on the wooden bench. I was thinking about Grisha, what he was doing.

Next time he came to the country, I decided I would have to talk to him. I would ask him to let me join the underground. I dreamed about giving my life to fighting against Stalin.

One evening Pietr Ivanovich caught up with me. "Do you mind if I join you?" He asked, and added, "Lately you don't come to the evening teas and I miss playing duets with you. You don't even practice piano anymore."

"I've a lot on my mind," I answered. We walked silently for a while.

"I guess I know what's wrong," Pietr Ivanovich said. "Not really wrong," he added, "I'd say it's rather right. At your young age it's obvious, of course, and I'd say all symptoms are very clear." He stopped talking and looked at me with embarrassment.

I was really puzzled. "Pietr Ivanovich, what are you talking about? What symptoms?"

We came to a bench. He sat down and invited me to join him. "Well, first of all, let's examine a few facts. You walk every evening alone in the garden. It seems you are miles away. There's melancholy in your eyes and face. Simple deduction—it's a matter of the heart," he said, joyfully observing my face. I did not know what to say and shrugged my shoulders. Looking at me inquiringly, he continued, obviously content with himself.

"Now, the question is who—Misha or Grisha?" He bent toward me and said quietly, "To tell the truth, I prefer Misha."

Finally, I understood and it was so funny I started laughing. "Oh, dear Pietr Ivanovich, you mean you think that I am, how to say it, romantically interested in one of the boys?"

"I thought that was the reason."

I stopped laughing and said sadly, "If you only knew how far from the truth you are. Life is hard. There are many things that I have to sort out and think over, to understand, and learn how to go ahead with my life."

"No romance?" He seemed to be disappointed.

"Romance is not for me," I said, standing up and smiling at the old man. "Thank you for making me laugh, and I promise we will play some duets tomorrow."

He also rose from the bench. "I guess I've been a fool. Will you forgive me?"

"Of course I will; you cured me. You see, the melancholy disappeared from my eyes," I joked.

Pietr Ivanovich's words gave me something to think about. What was my attitude towards Misha and Grisha? I was becoming attached to Misha. I looked forward to his coming on Sunday. He was a good friend, almost like Tonia. I felt calm and safe in his presence. Misha was solid.

Grisha, yes, what about Grisha? He was exactly the opposite—nervous, dissatisfied, unpredictable. I admired him for his convictions, for his willingness to fight for his beliefs: yes, better action and danger than passivity.

The second week of August was still hot and humid, and there were storms almost every night. I missed swimming in the river. But there was no lake, not even a stream where we lived. I had considered going to town to swim and realized it would be too dangerous. I must have looked forlorn and miserable because when Misha arrived on Sunday, he found me sitting on the steps leading to the verandah, and jeered good naturedly.

"Why such a sour face?"

"I am hot, I wish I could jump into some water."

Misha thought for a moment and said, "I think it could be arranged." He disappeared into the house. I heard him talking to Olga Petrovna. In a short while he was rolling a huge barrel from behind the house. He placed it close to the well (there was no plumbing in the house and water had to be brought from the deep well). The pail was lowered to the surface of the well and when filled, cranked up by hand.

"Here," Misha said laughingly. "All we have to do is fill it with water. You want to help?"

We both worked hard to fill the barrel, and it was so much fun. Then I put on my bathing suit (Misha borrowed one from dad), and we alternated jumping in and out, very quickly out because the water was ice cold. My parents, Olga Petrovna, and Pietr Ivanovich laughed watching us have a little happiness. I accepted it philosophically—one day at a time.

The next day in the late afternoon Natasha suddenly appeared. My heart skipped, bringing back horrible memories. She looked well and appeared to be happy. She came to say good-bye. They were ordered back to the Soviet Union, but she did not seem to mind. Mother and father invited her for tea.

"Boris has a new job in Kiev. I like this city and am glad we are going there," she said.

"But you liked it so much here. Isn't it a hardship for you to go back?" I asked.

"I did," she smiled, "but now it is time to go back." Natasha stayed for a while, telling my parents about her plans.

Finally she stood up. "I better catch the seven o'clock train." She added, "Lara, will you walk me to the station?"

I nodded.

For a while we walked through the fields in silence. Natasha looked around, breathing deeply. "Oh, Lara, how nice to be in the country. I hate cities. Here you are close to the earth. That's where the real meaning of life is." She stopped and picked up a handful of dirt, crushing it with her fingers. "Good earth, not sandy, good black soil." She sighed. "How I wish I had even a small plot of my own. How I would've worked on it." She looked at me and I saw despair in her eyes. "How could Stalin take our land away?"

I just shook my head. Even though trusting Natasha, I was afraid to say anything.

We resumed walking. After a while Natasha said quietly, "I am pregnant."

I was startled. "Pregnant? You mean you are going to have a baby?"

"Why do you have such scared eyes, Lara? Yes, I am going to have a baby, and this is the best thing that ever happened to me. For the eight years Boris and I were married, I hoped and hoped—and nothing. Oh, how I prayed for a child."

"Why are you telling me this?"

"Because the father of the child is the NKVD man."

"Oh, my God," I exclaimed with horror in my voice.

"It's all right, Lara, it's all right. He'll never know. That's why I am glad we are leaving town and I'll never see him again in my life."

"But your husband?"

"Oh, he will not know, either. I can't tell him. Don't you think we had enough hardship in our lives? We will raise the child together with lots of love."

"Why tell me your secret?" I asked again. I really did not understand her frankness.

She sighed and for a while we walked without speaking. Then she said very quietly, "Somehow I felt that you should know that from that terrible thing, something good happened. I believe it might help you to know."

I thought for a moment and said, "Yes, it would." I took her hand and squeezed it.

"God has his unpredictable ways, Natasha, doesn't He?"

We came to the station. I looked at Natasha. She was radiant; there was a glow in her face.

She smiled at me. "Now, dear girl, run home. I'll wait for the train by myself, and remember what I told you is between you and me."

"Yes, Natasha, it is between us only."

I came close to her and embraced her. For a moment, we held each other. I let go of her and said, "I wish you the best of everything. God bless you and your child."

"God bless you too, Lara."

I could feel tears coming to my eyes, so I gave her another hug and left. After a few paces I turned around. She saw me turn and waved at me. *I'm never going to see her again*, I thought.

24   NEW LODGINGS

For the next several days it rained steadily. Autumn was not too far off. Soon school would start. I would have to commute to the city. I dreaded that. It was so pleasant in the country away from propaganda. Mother was looking for a teaching job. Just 10 kilometers from our community was an interchange railroad station in a village with a population of less than five thousand. Mother applied there and soon had a position in a grade school. Now we started to look for new lodgings. It was not easy. Anything available was occupied by Soviet people. Finally we found a room, though it was much smaller than the one we had now—and there was no kitchen. Instead we had to put a small stove in the room. After we brought in our few pieces of necessary furniture, it was hard to move around. By the end of August we were already at our new place.

Misha helped us immensely. I don't know what we would have done without him, without his cheerfulness and caring. In a week, he had to leave for the university in the city of Lvov. There was still no word from Grisha. I asked Misha if he had seen him.

"Just occasionally," he said shortly. "But as you know, we don't see eye to eye." He looked at me and added, "Better stay away from Grisha, he is nothing but trouble."

"Because you don't understand him," I retorted.

"Oh, I understand him all right. He is a dreamer and idealist, and it is not the time for that." He thought for a moment and continued, "With his actions he can hurt not only himself, but others, too."

"What do you know about his actions?" I asked.

"I know enough."

"And you don't share his ideals?"

"Under the circumstances they are plain stupid and childish, Lara."

"Stupid, childish, Misha, how can you say that? I call them noble."

Misha shrugged his shoulders. "Let's not talk abut Grisha," he said.

I felt disappointed in Misha. *Well, before long I will see Grisha at school*, I thought.

September was approaching. It would soon be a year since the war started and Stalin occupied our territory. How many unbelievable changes occurred during the past twelve months! From a fine spacious house with the comfort of servants, we were now reduced to one small room in which we even had to cook. *Oh, Lara, how can you complain? Think about Tonia in Kazakstan*, I told myself.

The thought came to me. Yes, I was very fortunate to have the life I had before the war. But how about other people like our servant, Lida? She worked hard, cooking and cleaning with no prospect of improving her life, or our gardener, Nikolai? He and his wife had an old cottage, one room and a kitchen, with an earthen floor. Besides working part-time for my parents, he worked days in the city mill, getting only a couple of zlotys a day. His wife worked as a laundry woman. I knew they could barely make ends meet. And there were many other poor people in our town before the war. There were even beggars on the streets. I simply did not think about them before. Now I, too, had to experience hardship. But I really did not mind. I did not mind living in one room. What I minded was the loss of personal freedom — freedom to say what I thought, to do what I wanted, to express my opinions, even to criticize without the constant fear of being arrested.

And what about those poor people? Were they better off now? No, they were not. They had even less goods than they had before. The only difference now was that everybody was poor except the communist party officials.

I dreaded going back to school. During the two months in the country the pressure of Soviet rule had eased. I had rested a little bit morally, but I knew I was like an ostrich hiding its head in its feathers. Now I had to face reality. I thought about Tonia. Did she receive the package with the warm clothes?

Winter was coming. *How are they going to survive in an earth home?* I asked myself. Counting one month for the package to arrive and for her return letter to reach me. I could be hearing from her fairly soon. I hoped I could help her again.

Misha was supposed to come on Sunday for the last time before leaving for the university. I became used to his presence and I knew I would miss him. At school, however, I would see Grisha. He had become sort of a hero in my eyes. I was still dreaming of being part of the underground.

Sunday turned out to be sunny and warm. Misha came earlier than usual. Mother invited him for lunch. He was quiet and looked sad.

"What is wrong, Misha?" I asked.

He shrugged his shoulders. "Oh, I don't know, just not in a happy mood, I guess. Well, let's go for a walk, Lara, our last walk."

"Don't say 'last walk,' Misha. You will be back for Christmas."

"And we will walk in the snow." He smiled.

"Yes, we will," I agreed, but each of us was thinking that many things could happen in four months.

We followed the path to the woods. Leaves were starting to turn yellow and red, the air had that specific aroma of ripeness, decay and freshness all at the same time. The path was narrow and I walked ahead of Misha—we did not speak.

Finally we came to a small stream. I sat on a fallen log. "Let us rest for awhile," I said. Misha sat next to me and sighed. "What is wrong with you today?" I asked again. He did not answer. He seemed to be deep in his thoughts.

Finally he turned to face me and said slowly, "It is so hard for me to leave you here alone." He shook his head and stared into the woods, then continued after a pause. "I want you to know, Lara, how I feel about you. I thought about my feelings seriously and they are very strong. You are very important to me. Parting with you is hard, especially since I will be worried about you." He spoke slowly, articulating every word. He paused and continued.

"I just don't know how to handle my feelings." He turned to face me and I saw a pair of blue eyes looking so tenderly at me. He took my hand and was stroking it lightly. I froze inside and could not say a word.

"You look scared, Lara. Why?" He said gently. His face was so close to mine. Then he let go of my hand and put his arms around me, pulling me towards him. I felt his lips on my forehead, then on my lips. Suddenly I felt horrified. I pushed him with all my strength and jumped from the log.

"No, no." I was shouting. "Don't touch me, don't you ever touch me." I was shaking like a leaf. "You can't have any feelings for me, Misha, you can't, I don't deserve them."

Misha was startled. He got up from the log. "What is going on? I don't understand. Why such a strong reaction? All I wanted was to put my arms around you, a little kiss maybe—that's all."

I sensed hurt in his voice and felt even worse. "Misha listen to me. Oh, how can I explain this to you? I know you didn't mean any harm, but you see, I tried to forget a horrible thing that happened. I really tried to bury it very deep inside me. But I can't. It comes back to my mind and it hurts, and I know it will never go away. You see, that's why I want to join the underground." I looked at Misha and saw bewilderment in his face.

"Lara, you don't make any sense. You're scaring me."

"Misha, Misha, if you only knew." By now tears were streaming from my eyes. I tried to wipe them with my hands. "If you knew, you probably would not want to talk to me." Now he looked really worried.

"If I only knew what? What are you talking about? You don't deserve my feelings? What horrible thing happened? Lara, what's wrong? Tell me." He made a step toward me, but I jumped back.

Through tears I mumbled, "I am sorry, Misha. I better go home."

"You are not going anywhere until you explain everything. Here," he pulled a handkerchief from his pocket. "Wipe your face and calm down. We're going to talk."

I felt exhausted. Sitting on the log, I covered my face in my hands. Misha sat on the other end from me. A sudden uncontrollable urge to tell Misha overwhelmed me. Slowly I started talking and then it became easier and easier. It seemed by talking, I could get the poison out of my system. Misha listened in silence. When I came to the part where the NKVD man dumped me on the bed, he got up and I saw horror on his face. I stopped talking.

"Go on, go on. You've got to tell me everything," he said with a harsh voice.

So I told him how Natasha interrupted the man, about my talk with her, and how that night when I was ready to go to him, Natasha saved me again.

Misha was pacing back and forth in front of me. "Oh, my God, oh, my God," he was repeating.

When I finished he was standing in front of me, shaking his head. "My poor little girl, poor little girl. I just can't believe what you went through and kept it all to yourself. But, thank God, the worst did not happen. Bless Natasha. Oh, bless Natasha. And that man, oh, I could kill him, kill him with my bare hands."

He started pacing again. "Now, Lara, try to forget. Just block it from your mind. But how can I leave you? Now it will be even harder for me. What am I going to do?"

I got up from the log. I was tired, so tired. "Let's go back, Misha."

We were facing each other. His face was flushed. "How can I leave you, how can I go away now?" He kept repeating. There was despair in his voice.

I felt sad and resigned. "Each of us has a life to live, Misha," I said, and added, "We better hurry. You have a train to catch."

We walked silently, each of us trying to understand what just happened. I felt somehow closer to Misha now. Soon we came to the train station. I looked at the clock on the building.

"You still have fifteen minutes," I said.

"Fifteen minutes," he repeated sadly.

It was funny, but now I felt stronger than Misha. I could see how sad he was. We sat on the bench the sun was already behind the trees. We talked a little bit about his university and my school. Misha warned me to be very careful.

"Don't trust anybody. Don't confide in anybody. I will write to you and you be careful what you write to me."

"I will be careful, Misha, I will." But I understood all the hopelessness of our lives, and I knew we would never be able to adjust to Stalin's society. The train was coming. We got up from the bench and went up on the platform. It was time to part. I extended my hand to Misha. He held it for a moment then quickly kissed it and let go. Stepping into the train, he said, "Remember how I feel about you!"

I stood on the platform until the train was out of sight. Then slowly I went home. Another page of my life had turned.

25   BACK TO SCHOOL & TO THE CITY

With Misha's departure I felt a void. I was thinking about our recent meeting in the woods: his caring so much for me, my confession. I was so glad I told him everything.

On the first day of school I woke up with a funny feeling in my stomach.

I was scared to face school and, most of all, the city. Assuming we would survive that long, I had one more year until graduation. I tried to visualize my future once I graduated from high school. With the 11th paragraph label placed on me and my parents as enemies of the State, I was not allowed to live in any big city where I would be able to attend a university. Thus, I was denied the opportunity for a higher education. Moreover, as we were registered in the village where we lived, we were not permitted to leave. There was a special word used by the Soviets, *prikreplon*, meaning place-bound.

Less than 100 years ago, Tzar Alexander abolished serfdom in Russia; now Stalin was trying to enslave the people once again.

Mother's hand touched my hair.

"Lara, it is time to get up."

"I hate to go back to the city, mama," I said quietly.

"Lara, you have only one year to graduation. I know, dearest, how hard this city is for you and if I only could..." Her voice cracked. I jumped out of bed and embraced her.

"Mama, dear mama. I am sorry, so sorry. Forgive me, I'm so selfish." We stood there clinging to each other.

"Lara," she said softly, "get ready for school. Go, study—whatever knowledge you gather will help you cope with life."

The train to the city left at seven o'clock. Half an hour ride and a twenty-minute walk brought me to school before eight o'clock, and on time.

The morning was cool with a cloudless sky. *The day will be warm*, I thought. On the platform there were quite a few people, several children. Some were local and some obviously from the Soviet Union— children of the occupying force.

One girl caught my eye. Tall, very thin with blond hair plaited in one long braid, she must have been my age. I could not see her eyes. *They must be blue or gray*, I thought. There was some assertiveness in her posture. She looked around with curiosity. Our eyes met, she smiled at me—I turned my face away. *Why did you do that? That was not nice of you, Lara*, I said to myself. The train was coming and I rushed to the compartment. The girl followed me and sat on the opposite bench.

After a while looking straight at me she said, "My name is Olga. Today is my first day in this city."

I knew I had to say something so I asked, "Where did you live before?"

"In Moscow," she answered. "I was born there." Her voice was very melodic and friendly. She smiled. Obviously she wanted to continue the conversation.

Suddenly I felt instant sympathy toward her. This time I smiled back.

"My name is Lara, it's an abbreviation from Larisa. What school are you going to?" I asked. She named her school. "It is mine, too," I said.

"Oh, how nice," she exclaimed. "Can I walk with you? I really don't know the way."

"Sure," I said feeling a little bit uneasy. On the way to school we talked, that is, she talked and I listened.

I learned that she was seventeen, a senior, just like me. Her father had been sent to the occupied zone to work.

"What kind of work does your father do?" I asked.

"He was sent here to help local people with the collectivization of their farms. Poor papa."

Then she added. "He has a hard time with those peasants, they resist. Can you imagine, they dare to resist! Why can't they understand the necessity of collectivization and farming on state farms?"

I could not help asking, "Necessity of state farms? Why can't peasants simply farm their own land?"

She shook her head, "So you don't understand it either?"

"School is only a couple of blocks away, Olga," I said, wanting to stop unpleasant conversation, but she probably did not even hear me.

She seemed deep in thought. After a while she spoke as in a trance. "Look, Lara, we're building socialism to pave the way to communism." She paused and then continued. "That is the future, of course, and you people will have to learn." There was hardness in her voice.

So this is the Soviet, not Russian, generation, I said to myself, *brainwashed from the cradle*.

At school we learned that although we were both seniors, we had different classes. *Thank God for that*, I thought. The mood at school was different from previous years. Before the occupation there was much gaiety and laughter. Classmates were happy to see friends they missed during the summer months. There was always much to talk about, to share. Now the mood was somber. I noticed that even more portraits of Lenin and Stalin appeared on the walls. It was the communist custom to decorate classes and halls with red banners and slogans. It only gave me the feeling that the walls were plastered with blood.

I looked for Grisha, but could not find him anywhere. He must have been assigned to classes that were different from mine. During recess I finally spotted him in the hall, standing alone looking out through a window. I came close and touched his elbow. He turned towards me and said simply, "Oh, it's you, Lara."

I looked at him and felt my throat squeeze. He looked so haggard. But there was more maturity in his features. His face was tan and handsome.

"Hi, Grisha, I was looking for you. I've not seen you for so long. I hoped you would visit me in the country during the summer. I missed you," I said.

Grisha looked at me sadly but kindly, even smiled a little. His hand touched my cheek.

"Was it a good summer? You look healthy, rested, much better than in the spring," his voice became more friendly.

"Yes, summer helped me a lot. I feel more mature. I think you can trust me now," I said pleadingly.

"Lara, here you go again." He seemed annoyed.

"Grisha, no matter what you say, I still think you can let me—" I said it all in one breath, but he interrupted me.

"Stop, not a word." And looking around suspiciously added in a low voice, "Lara, listen and listen good. I want you to stay away from me. I don't want you to have any contact with me. It is dangerous for you."

"So it is true that..." I couldn't finish. His face flashed with anger.

"My God, these naive girls," he exclaimed. And lowering his face to mine, said in a whisper, "Just leave me alone. I hope you can understand that— leave me alone," he repeated and pushing me aside, left. I felt so hurt. I watched him walk away, along the hall until he disappeared around the corner. Tears filled my eyes.

Now, Lara, you want to cry, little baby, I whispered. *Control yourself, girl, no wonder Grisha thinks you are immature and naive.*

The bell rang for the next class. I knew for sure now that Grisha was mixed up with some kind of a Polish resistance group. I felt a surge of admiration for him and at the same instance thought myself little and insignificant. Sadly I returned to class.

Life fell into a routine: morning rides on the train six days of school—Sunday off. There were no services on Sunday because churches were still closed. My evenings were filled with homework and piano practice. I read voraciously. Books transported me into a different world, helped me to understand many things, and most of all helped me to cope with the present.

Weeks passed. Mother continued her teaching at the local school. Father's job was to obtain food by standing in lines (by now we were used to lines) that consumed quite a bit of time, and gave him something to do. Occasionally, Vasia and his mother would come to visit. Through them we heard about arrests of more local people. Our former house was now entirely occupied by the NKVD man and his family.

I saw Grisha almost every day, but I made a point not to come near him. Sometimes he was in the company of a heavy-set girl, with short, brown hair. Her facial features were not attractive, but her eyes compensated for this defect. Long, dark lashes fringed her large, hazel eyes and gave soft shadows to her cheeks. When she smiled, a subtle warmth emanated from her face. Her name was Martha. She was in my class—a top student. I liked her very much. Her father, a wealthy landowner in Poland, was arrested during the first wave of arrests. Their property was confiscated and she and her mother were renting a room somewhere. Obviously Grisha trusted her.

A couple of times I tried to start a conversation with Martha, but got only short, polite answers. I felt ashamed of myself. I understood that I wanted, like a child, to play with conspiracy. But what about Grisha? What could he do against communist power? Was it not childish, too? Sooner or later he and his associates would be discovered. He probably knew that, but he chose resistance rather than submission. It was a protest, *I may perish but I won't bend.* I tried to examine my feelings for him. In my mind he was a hero.

I studied the best I could. Political studies were the hardest for me. Special teachers sent from the Soviet Union were assigned to indoctrinate students in the philosophy of communism. We had to study the works of Marx, Engels, Lenin, and Stalin. I hated it. I noticed children from the Soviet Union genuinely believed in Stalin's genius. For them he was a god. I recalled Voltaire's words, *If God did not exist he should be invented.*

Communists tried to abolish faith in God and instead were giving Stalin to the masses. Uniformity of thought was imposed by every possible means in the minds of children. From kindergarten on, they were taught to chant rhymes to the health of great communist leaders. The teachers, themselves, probably did not realize that they sounded like broken records. They constantly tried to persuade students that life under Stalin had become better — that life had become more joyful. *Stalin is thinking about everyone of us,* they parroted.

It was sickening for me to hear this constant propaganda. I hated living with the constant fear of being arrested and deported. I loathed such a controlled society.

Olga, my first day train companion, was a product of Soviet upbringing. As a child she belonged to the Pioneers and now to the Comsomols (the Communist Youth Organization). She thought and believed that in other countries people were dropping dead in the streets from hunger. She told me several times that, *yes, they had shortages of food and merchandise now, but the country was in transition. In her mind, enemies and saboteurs were everywhere. Contra-revolutionaries had to be weeded out, destroyed or resettled.*

I thought, *what kind of contra-revolutionaries were Tonia, her mother and brother?*

Olga always had a happy disposition. She laughed, joked often and teased me about my gloomy mood. Many times she asked me to tell her about my life in Poland.

"Lara, you always avoid my questions. I don't even know why you and your parents moved to this village. I know you lived in the city before, and you're always sad. Sometimes I see fear in your eyes. Why?"

But how could I explain to her my former comfortable life in a society free from terror? A time when we had freedom of speech, movement, freedom of choice. It was dangerous for me to praise my former life, and did I dare open her eyes? She was happy and satisfied with the present. I often joked, "Olga, don't make me talk about my past. You might become as sad as I am."

Despite here shallow mind, I really liked this bright, curious young girl. I became used to riding on the train with her and walking to school together even if I had to watch every word.

It was already the end of November and, like in previous years, the temperature dropped below freezing. Bitter cold enveloped the region. It snowed continuously. Commuting to school was not easy as a result. The train compartments were cold and the walk to school in the wind and snow was bitter. I often thought about Tonia. It must be even colder where she was. How could she and her family survive the winter in an earth house?

I wondered if she received the package Grisha and I sent. It was painful to think about Tonia. I hoped I would get a letter someday.

Twice a week after regular school I went to my music school. On one of those days, right before I entered the conservatory building, a hand grabbed my elbow. Startled, I turned around and came face to face with Grisha. I barely recognized him with his hat pulled almost to his eyebrows and his coat collar covering his chin as if he wanted to hide his face.

"Grisha, is that you?" I almost choked.

"Lara," he said, "I know you have a lesson now, but after the lesson would you have time? I have to talk to you. It's urgent."

"Yes, Grisha, I usually have forty-five minutes before I catch the train," I answered quickly.

"Good, then after your lesson go straight to the station and wait for me. Go inside the building and when you see me, follow me, but don't come close, just follow." Without another word, he left.

My God, Grisha finally wanted to talk to me. I was so excited. *About what,* I wondered. Something must have happened.

During the lesson I could barely concentrate. My teacher and I were practicing Mozart's piano concerto in A-minor—on two pianos. "Dear child, what is wrong with you?" My teacher asked. I just looked at her, feeling guilty.

After what seemed like ages, the lesson was over and I rushed to the station. It was already after four o'clock and getting dark. *Must have been below zero,* I thought, but I did not feel the cold. A thousand thoughts went through my mind. I almost ran. Finally at the railroad station I entered the building. It was early. Only a few people sat in the waiting room.

No sign of Grisha. Well, he told me to wait for him. I was getting more nervous. *Lara, calm yourself, calm yourself,* I was repeating to myself.

A thousand thoughts went through my mind.

Then he was there. Grisha entered the waiting room. Like he asked, I did not approach him. For a while he pretended to look at the schedule, then left. I waited a little bit so it would not be obvious, and then left, too. The snow had begun to fall again. In the dim glow of a lantern I could make out Grisha standing by the corner of a building.

The minute he noticed my presence he moved toward a long line of boxcars that were parked at a distance from the main building. He stopped again.

I followed cautiously. Soon I could not see him anymore. I reached the first boxcar and did not know where to go. Visibility was poor.

"Lara, here, behind this car," Grisha's voice was strained. I took a couple of steps and there he was with the hat pulled over his eyebrows and a scarf over his mouth. My heart was pounding.

"You wanted to see me," I said in a faint voice. Without answering, he reached into his pocket and pulled out an envelope.

"Here, put it in your pocket quickly, otherwise it will get wet."

Automatically I did what he told me and then asked, "What is this?"

"A letter from Tonia."

"From Tonia!" I exclaimed.

"Shhh. Please be quiet, Lara. Yes, I got the letter yesterday and this is your part of it. She wrote to me, too, but it's personal."

"How is she?"

"They are alive so far," Grisha answered in a sad voice. "They made it through the summer somehow, but now the cold months are coming. Tonia's mother is very sick. If they stay in that same place... They won't make it through the winter."

"Did Tonia get our package?" I had to know.

"Yes, she did, and it helped, but now she has a big decision to make." I detected pain and even anger in his voice.

"What decision? Tell me!"

"Read the letter, Lara, and you will understand. Worst of all, I can't help her." His voice cracked. I moved closer to Grisha and put my arm on his shoulder.

"Oh, Grisha." That was all I could say. Suddenly he grabbed me and I was in his arms.

"It hurts, Lara, it hurts so much." He was pressing against me, as if asking for sympathy. I embraced him tightly. A good, warm feeling spread over my whole body. Grisha needed me.

I don't know how long we stood there in the falling snow holding each other. Then Grisha pulled back. "I should get a hold of myself," he said, "and you have a train to catch."

"Wait, Grisha, what about the letter? Can we write to her?"

"Yes, there is a new address on the envelope. You write, I will not." He paused and added, "Tell her I'll always pray for her."

I could not go without asking, "Can I talk to you again, maybe... Sometimes?"

Without answering my question, he said, "Go now. When you enter the building I will leave."

We were standing very close to each other. It was hard for me to go. I wanted to comfort him, to say a few warm words. "Grisha," I said pleadingly, "if I could only help."

"Oh, dear girl," he sighed, "you helped me already by being here, and I know you care." His voice was full of sorrow.

He hesitated for a moment and then took my wet face in both hands and I felt his lips on my forehead.

Then he released me. "Hurry, Lara, or you'll miss the train."

I knew I had to. As soon as I left the shelter of the boxcar, wind and snow hit my face. Struggling, I reached the station. People were already boarding the train. I rushed to the platform and stepped on.

At this time there were only a few passengers and I easily found an empty compartment. I had to read Tonia's letter. Briskly brushing the snow from my hat and coat, I sat down, and closed my eyes. I felt emotionally and physically exhausted. A shrill whistle sounded, doors slammed and the train lurched forward.

26   Tonia's Letter

Carefully reaching into my pocket I retrieved the letter. It was slightly wet. The envelope was made of brownish paper. It had Grisha's address on it and on the back the name and address of a person unknown to me. It bore a man's name.

Dear Lara, it said, *I hope this letter will reach you and Grisha.*

I looked at the date on the top right hand corner. *She wrote this letter almost two months ago,* I realized. I kept on reading.

I would like to thank you both for your package. It helped a lot, especially the tea. I went to the nearby village and exchanged it for other food items. We are still alive, but mother is weak and Andrei, so skinny. He is always hungry. Winter is coming. It was hard enough in the summer. Mother and I had to work in the fields. Lara, you should see me now, my face is burned by the sun, my hands covered with wounds. My whole body hurts. I am tired, I am so tired. I run sometimes into the fields and shout as loud as I can from the top of my lungs. Am I going crazy?

A couple of months ago I met a young man in the village. He was very kind to all of us. Thanks to him we did not starve. Now he wants to marry me. Then we could all go and live in the village with his family. Andrei could go to school. We would be warm.

Remember our dreams? The knight on the white horse? How childish I was then. Lara, I don't want to marry this man. I don't love him, but do I have a choice? I don't care for myself, but what about mama and Andrei? Winter in this earth house? They won't survive. I pray to God to give me strength. Lara, please write to me. I often think of you. I hope all of you are all right. The address on the envelope is the address of the young man. I embrace you my dear friend. Please pray for us as I always pray for you.

  With love,
  Tonia

The hand holding the letter dropped to my knee. *So Tonia is married by now,* I whispered. I was sure that was what she did. Submitted herself to the man she did not love, and maybe even resented. My poor friend. I thought about our girlish talks. We promised ourselves to marry only that chosen one, and save ourselves for the wedding night. We had read too many mushy books with such endings. Where couples looked into each other's eyes and their souls melted into one. *It was a lifetime ago. We were young, naive girls.* I sighed.

A peaceful thought came to my mind. *The young man will take care of Tonia and her family. They'll not be hungry or cold. My God, how life had changed from previous years.* To be glad because we were not hungry or cold? We were really spoiled in our childhood, Tonia and I.

I closed my eyes. The rhythmic noise of the running train, the warmth of the compartment, soothed me. I was drifting with my thoughts. The Greek word *pantarei* came to my mind. I heard it from my religion teacher some years ago and it fascinated me.

The rhythmic noise of the running train soothed me.

I recalled how he said it was hard to translate that word; it refers to the flow and passing of life. *Life is like a river*, the priest explained. *Sometimes smooth and calm, sometimes turbulent, deep or shallow, treacherous or gentle, unpredictable. It flows constantly, changeable, like life itself.*

A rough voice brought me to reality. "Hey, girl, what are you doing? Do you want to stay on the train overnight? Disembark and fast."

I opened my eyes and saw the conductor. Quickly I gathered my belongings and got off the train. The snow had stopped falling. I was glad to see my mother. When I took a later train she always came to meet me. She rushed towards me. I heard her exclaim, "Are you all right? I was so worried."

I snuggled against her, murmuring *mama, mama.*

"What took you so long to get off the train, Lara?"

"I fell asleep, I was so tired," I said simply, and then added, "I got a letter from Tonia."

Mother let out a sigh. "How are they?"

"They are alive," I answered, "I'll tell you everything when we get home." Walking home was not easy. During the day several inches of new snow had fallen. In some places it reached our ankles.

But the air was fresh, frosty, almost enticing. I looked around. It was like an enchanted world. The village was surrounded by a deep forest. Friendly lights shone nearby in the cottages. Under the light of the street lanterns, snow glistened like tiny jewels. In the dark night, millions of stars winked at me mysteriously, and there was a crescent moon right above snow-covered pine trees. I gazed at the slender crescent. A full moon was cold and indifferent. Its old face was saying, "I know it all." A new moon was friendly and warm, reminding me of Gogol's tale *The Night Before Christmas*. The cover had a picture of a devil sitting on a crescent moon and a witch riding a broom through the dark skies. It was a funny and exciting story about a devil stealing the moon and all the commotion it caused.

Suddenly I stopped and shouted, "Hey, moon, do you know the word pantarei?"

Startled, mother turned toward me. "Lara, to whom are you talking?"

"I am talking to the moon, mama," I said, cheerily. "You see, it is playing peek-a-boo with me. Now it's hiding, but if I move this way I can see it again." Unexpectedly, I had an overwhelming desire to laugh.

"Ha, ha, ha, moon, moon, peek-a-boo, you can see me and I can see you!"

"You silly, silly girl, what got into you?" Mother asked, but looking at me jumping in the snow she became high-spirited, too.

It was a relief to laugh—I had not laughed for such a long time. Finally, I calmed down. "You know, mama, it is better to laugh than cry, because after all everything is pantarei." I almost sang. Mother shook her head.

"Lara, let's go home. Father is waiting with warm soup."

"Soup? What kind?" I felt a pang of hunger.

"Split pea, even with meat."

"Oh, good, it's my favorite."

Shortly, we were home.

Father was anxiously waiting for us with a hot meal. It was simple, but nourishing, soup, bread, and Mama had baked an apple cake for dessert.

I read Tonia's letter aloud. "Sad, very sad," papa said, shaking his head, "but let's hope she will find some kind of happiness or contentment in her future." I noticed that father seemed to be a little nervous.

"Papa, are you all right?"

He lowered his voice and said, "Vasia and his mother visited us this afternoon. Vasia had quite interesting news." Papa's eyes were sparkling.

"Is he still listening on the shortwave radio?"

"He is, and it's dangerous to listen to Western broadcasting, but you know Vasia, he has to know what is going on beyond the Iron Curtain, beyond this communist state."

I became excited. For a whole summer we were kept in the dark regarding world news. Listening to the Soviet radio with all its propaganda was nauseating; the same applied to official newspapers. Moreover, the news was always distorted. But now, after listening to the British shortwave radio, Vasia brought us the news that in May, Hitler invaded Holland and Belgium, pushed part of his army through Luxembourg, and reached the French border.

French and English forces were unable to withstand the German superiority and on June 22nd, the French government of Marchal Petain signed surrender papers. Paris with all its treasures was declared an open city. After securing himself in most of Western Europe, Hitler ordered air strikes against England.

"So Hitler is going to invade England now?" I asked.

Father paused a little and then said, "No, not England, he will just bomb England, but I'm sure he will invade Russia, that is, the Soviet Union," he corrected himself.

"Papa, what are you saying?" I exclaimed, "Hitler will start war here?"

"My dear girl, it was always Germany's goal to move eastward. You know the expression, *Drung nach Osten—push to the East.* Hitler needs colonies and slaves."

"Papa, papa, but that means," I was almost out of breath, I was so excited, "that means Hitler can destroy communism. If France and England could not resist how can Stalin?"

"Do you think fascism is any better? Don't forget Hitler means to enslave other nations," papa said poignantly.

"But not our souls," I retorted. "Here we are like reptiles, crawling on the ground, compelled to sing praises to that monster, Stalin. Anything will be better than the present." I raised my voice. "Sometimes I think I can't take it anymore."

"Shh." Mother interrupted, "enough discussions. Lara, you had a long day. Time to go to bed."

Falling asleep, I repeated to myself, *Maybe there is hope for us to survive.*

I now understood Grisha and why he was in the underground. In case of war he would fight the communists, actually fight! *Why didn't he want me beside him?* I fell asleep with his name on my lips.

27   OLGA

The next day at school I could not concentrate on my work. In my natural state of resignation there had appeared a small bright spot, a hope that communism might be destroyed. Who would destroy it and what would come afterward was not important to me. One evil would be gone.

I hated Stalin to the point of obsession. I believed that given a chance to kill him, I would do it without hesitation. I often imagined myself in the Kremlin, a gun in my hand. I would find Stalin and then pull the trigger; shoot and shoot. Was I capable of murder?

That morning on the train I was not very friendly to Olga. As always, she was asking too many questions! I had too much on my mind. Tonia's letter, my meeting with Grisha, and hope filled my thoughts. I could hardly wait for school to end.

The day was a Saturday, which meant early dismissal. After school I rushed to the station. I walked quickly, trying to avoid Olga. On the train I found an empty compartment, sat down and closed my eyes. I wanted to be alone with my thoughts, to quietly sort out my feelings.

Sure enough, however, Olga found me. "Here you are," I heard her voice, "I was looking for you. You acted rather strangely this morning, Lara." She sat down on the bench across from me, looking inquiringly into my eyes and smiling.

I really had no desire to talk to her, but I had to say something.

"I was just thinking about many things."

"Thinking about what?"

I hesitated a moment and then lied. "I was thinking about graduation this spring and the year ahead."

"Oh, yes." Olga sighed. "Can you imagine next fall we will be in college?"

You will be in college, not I, I thought and asked, "What subjects are you going to take?"

"I like math," Olga answered eagerly, "so engineering will be my goal. Structural engineering, maybe," she added. "Our country needs to build more factories and other industrial buildings."

And more concentration camps, I said sarcastically in my mind. I asked, "And after college, in what part of the Soviet Union would you like to settle and work?"

She raised her eyebrows. "What part of the country? Silly Lara, I will have to go where the party sends me."

Now I was surprised, "You would *have* to go!" I emphasized the word "have." "What if it is some remote part of the Soviet Union and you would not want to be separated from your family?"

She shook her head. "I wouldn't dare refuse."

"But what if it is going to be for the rest of your life?" I was pressing. Olga seemed to be annoyed.

"I'll work where I'm sent," she said decisively. "Stalin knows where I'm most needed."

The train was rolling. I did not reply. I looked through the window at the passing scenery, fields covered with snow, a line of trees in the background. It was sunny. Not a cloud in the sky. *Already December*, I thought, *in two weeks we'll have our winter break. Misha'll come home from college.* Somehow I had almost forgot about him. Misha, such a good friend.

I looked at Olga—she stared ahead, apparently deep in her own thoughts. Now I asked, "What are you thinking about, Olga?"

She stirred. "I was thinking about what you said, and I wondered how it used to be in Poland. Weren't students, after graduation, placed in positions where the government wanted them to be?"

"No, there was no compulsory placement. The government didn't interfere with our private lives." Olga looked at me in disbelief. I went on, "Students had the choice of going where they wanted to, you know, where suitable jobs were available. There was freedom of movement in Poland." The minute I said these words, I regretted them.

"It's very interesting what you say, Lara, providing you are telling me the truth," she said dryly.

I knew I was on dangerous ground. I shook my head. "Oh, Olga, I was just joking."

She shrugged her shoulders. "Sometimes I don't think you were joking." She paused and then said, "You know, you're a mystery to me. I would like to know why you are always so sad. Maybe I can help. I want to be your friend."

There was sincerity in her voice. The blue eyes smiled at me, but that aggravated me even more and I retorted, "Don't ask questions, Olga, because if you knew the truth," I said laughingly, "you might get sad eyes like I have." She touched my arm with her hand.

"Listen, Lara, please understand I'm new here in this liberated territory." Again she said *liberated.* "I want to know more about your life here. You say something interesting and then make a joke out of it. I don't know what to believe." I kept silence, so she went on. "I have a feeling you are avoiding me altogether."

Definitely, Olga was getting on my nerves and I said angrily, "Yes, you are right. I'm trying to avoid you. I'm glad you noticed, and believe me it would be better for you not to associate with me, we are from two different worlds."

Olga looked puzzled. "Now you got me completely confused."

"Please," I said pleadingly, "let us stop this conversation. I'm quite tired."

She looked at me and sighed. "All right, if you wish, but just tell me one thing. Are you going to take music in college?"

Oh, God, why would she not leave me alone? "I'm not going to college. I'm not allowed go to college," I said quietly.

Olga was surprised. "Not allowed go to college! But why?"

I could feel I was losing control of my emotions. "Well, Olga, if you insist," I said, looking straight into her eyes, "this spring the eleventh paragraph was added to my parent's passports. They were labeled enemies of the communist state. We were thrown out of our house, which was nationalized. We're not allowed to live anywhere where the population is over five thousand people, and, as you know, colleges are only in big cities. Anyway, as a daughter of enemies of your country, I am not allowed to enter college." I spoke slowly articulating every word. She looked at me speechless. I continued, "Last winter my father was arrested, held in prison for a week, interrogated constantly. He collapsed mentally. He was a brilliant lawyer in Poland, and now he is a broken man." I stopped, exhausted.

"Your parents must have done something wrong," Olga said faintly. "They were probably rich and exploited the people."

"My father defended people, helped whoever was in need, and you say rich. Is this a crime?" I asked. I knew I had to stop this conversation, but I had said too much already, and I went on. "Whatever my parents had, they worked hard to achieve. After the revolution they came to Poland with just two suitcases."

"Aha," Olga interrupted, "your parents ran away, deserted their country. They should have stayed and helped to build communism."

"Helped build communism? Is this what you are doing here now with arrests of hundreds of people, with deportation of thousands?"

"What deportations?" Olga asked nervously.

"Oh! You don't know about deportation?" I was almost shouting. "Just listen. The first deportation was in February, the second in April. Innocent people were abducted in the wee hours of the night without any warning, packed into cattle wagons, sent to Siberia—men, women and children. Thirty persons to the wagon, three months on the road, half of them died." I was talking fast; nothing could stop me now although I knew I was signing my own death warrant.

"Just listen, Olga. I had a dear friend, Tonia. We grew up together, I loved her, her mother, little brother, all three of them were sent to Kazakstan."

I took a deep breath. Olga was looking at me speechless. I went on. "I got a letter from Tonia yesterday. You want to read it?"

"I don't know why you are telling me all this," Olga said hesitantly.

"But you wanted to know about my life, did you not? Here." My hands were trembling when I took Tonia's letter from my purse. Reluctantly she took the letter. I watched her reading it. Turmoil was in my head.

You wanted to know about my life, did you not?

Giving it back to me she said, "Deportation, arrests, concentration camps, but you must understand we are a new country. Stalin has to be careful. There are enemies, saboteurs, contra-revolutionaries everywhere."

"Yet it is justifiable to put millions in concentration camps? Millions of innocent people?"

Olga shrugged. "For the good of the future, for the ideals of communism, sacrifices have to be made."

"Slogans, slogans," I retorted.

Olga's face flushed. "Wait, Lara, wait. You said innocent people were persecuted, but look what you are doing now. Your words are contra-revolutionary, you're against Stalin, you criticize the action of the government. This is subversive, *you* are the enemy." She emphasized the word "you."

With an effort I calmed myself down and said slowly, "So you think I'm an enemy, contra-revolutionary, a saboteur, perhaps?" A smile crossed my lips. "Well, then you have to expose me. As soon as we get off the train you have to go directly to the NKVD office and tell them everything I said to you. That should be enough to have me arrested, shot, or sent to a concentration camp."

Olga looked at me horrified. "Lara, what are you saying? Are you out of your mind? How could I report you?"

"But weren't you taught from childhood to watch for signs of contra-revolution, to report anything said against the system? Remember the boy, Morosow, he was made a hero because he exposed his parents (he heard them criticizing Stalin) and they were shot?"

"Yes, I remember," she said faintly, shaking nervously. "But loyalty to the government should be above feelings for parents."

I took a deep breath and continued, "Now is your chance to be a hero, Olga."

She shook her head. "Oh, Lara, what are you doing to me? I'm completely confused." I noticed her eyes were filling with tears, her lower lip started to tremble.

The train was slowing down. I started to pick up my things. Before I left the compartment I turned to Olga. Now the tears were running down her cheeks. She was wiping them with her hands. *She doesn't even have a handkerchief*, I thought. I reached into my coat pocket and gave her mine.

"Wipe your tears and do what you were taught to do," I said cruelly, "and keep the handkerchief as a souvenir."

I stormed out of the train compartment realizing that I did something irreversibly terrible to Olga and myself. I left the train and started walking rapidly, filled with anger and frustration.

The cold, frosty air was pleasant to breathe. Sun rays reflecting from the white snow were blinding. Thoughts of despair were flying through my mind. *My God, what have I done?* In the last half an hour I managed to destroy any hope for survival, and I put a tremendous burden on an innocent naive girl who had been happy and content under the conditions she learned to accept since childhood.

My bottled-up feelings had exploded. Yet I had no right to ruin someone else's life. I knew Olga had no choice but to report everything I said. To conceal it would be dangerous to her. But could she live with the thought that I would perish because of her? I had shattered Olga's peaceful world. My cruel words, "Do your duty," were ringing in my ears. Her face, with the tears running down her cheeks, her words, "Lara, what are you doing to me?" Haunted me.

I thought of my parents. They, too, would perish with me. Self-hate filled me. What had I done? Strength was leaving me. I slowed down my walking pace. The path led me through a forest. I saw a fallen tree covered with snow and sat down. I looked around. The scene was peace—trees, white snow, the sun bright. I lifted my face to its rays. They felt kind and gentle. I closed my eyes and started praying. I did not ask God for help. I asked Him to forgive me. Slowly a sense of peace enveloped me. I put my head down and said to myself, *Lara, it is done, and nothing you can do about it.* I repeated this phrase until I felt a numbness inside me.

The sun moved behind the trees. I felt the cold. Getting up, I slowly went home. Snow under my feet rasped a crisp, crackling sound.

Right now I am free, I thought. *Tomorrow will be different. I will be in prison.* The arrests were always done after midnight.

Now I have to face my parents. How could I tell them what I did? Then I remembered that this was a Saturday and mother was out teaching Russian to railroad workers. She would return after six o'clock. So now only my father was home. Deep down, I knew somehow I would not have the courage to tell my parents what transpired between Olga and me.

In the small pantry leading to our quarters, I took off my overshoes and opened the door. A fire was burning in the stove. Father was sitting at a table reading a book. When he saw me, he got up. His face lit with a smile.

"There you are, dear girl, I was waiting for you. You must be frozen, it's very cold today."

"Very cold," I repeated his words.

"Give me your coat and come close to the stove. I have some warm milk for you."

"Thank you, papa," I said quietly with a lump in my throat. I could feel that he sensed something.

"Anything wrong, Lara?" He asked after a pause. I shook my head warming my hands over the stove's surface. Papa sighed, poured milk into a cup and handed it to me, saying, "There's bread and jam in the cupboard. We'll eat supper after mama gets home."

"Milk is all I need, thank you." I sipped the hot liquid with pleasure. Then, forcing myself to look straight into father's eyes, I said, "I'm so tired, so tired, papa, maybe I can lie down for a while?"

"Sure, child, sure, that's what you need, rest. I'll get you a pillow and a blanket." Then, looking laughingly at me, he added, "But first take off your scarf and hat, which, as a matter of fact, sits crookedly on your head." Trying to smile, I handed both items to him and lay down on the couch. Papa covered me with the blanket. For a moment his hand rested on my head.

"Sleep little one," he whispered. I closed my eyes, trying to make my mind a blank.

After a while, I felt as if I were falling into a deep black hole. Sound sleep enveloped me. Peace.

28   A NIGHT OF FEAR

I must have slept for several hours, then, I became aware that something was bringing me back into consciousness. *What was that? Aha, voices.* I could hear two voices. *Oh, please, leave me be. I don't want to come back to reality*, I pleaded silently, but the voices kept bothering me.

Mother's voice. "We have to wake her up, it is past seven o'clock. We have to eat supper."

Papa's voice. "She was pretty tired when she came home from school—she looked exhausted. I have a feeling something bad happened."

"Did she say anything?" Mama's voice betrayed an anxiousness.

Papa was quick to reply. "No, just that she wanted to rest."

"Did she eat anything?"

Poor papa, all these questions. "I poured her a glass of warm milk, that was all she wanted."

Mama insisted. "I have to wake her up." A soft hand touched my forehead and I opened my eyes.

"Mama."

She sat down on the couch next to me and said with a smile, "Hey, Sleeping Beauty, time to wake up, otherwise you won't be able to sleep through the night."

Mother's face was so kind. There was so much love emanating from her. I gave her a kiss on the cheek and got up.

Father was warming the food on the stove. I felt suddenly hungry. I had not eaten since lunch at school.

When we sat down for the meal I told myself, *Eat, Lara, eat, who knows when your next meal will be.* We made small talk at the table, but I could not look into my parent's eyes.

They tried to find out if anything was wrong, but I said I was just tired because it had been a long week.

Trying to stretch time before going to bed and to avoid further questions, I began to play the piano. Chopin nocturnes. How they suited my mood. Melancholy, deep in thought, dark in color. Chopin knew he had an incurable disease; he knew he was dying. I suddenly could connect to his pain. I forgot myself in the music, in the beauty of expression.

Finally I glanced at the clock on the piano. It was past ten. My parents were already in bed, asleep. Silently I prepared my bed and turned off the light.

Two more hours and I could expect the knock on the door, soldiers. *I should sleep with my clothes on,* I said to myself. I did not want to dress in front of the men who would come to arrest me. I slipped under the covers after removing only my skirt. I could not imagine what would happen to me in prison. I remembered the encounter with the NKVD man and Natasha's words. *Any man who will want to, will have you.* No, no, I did not want to think about that, it was better to think about my childhood, my wonderful childhood. I went back in time trying to recall the happy moments, but my ears were listening to all the sounds of the night.

The wind was picking up. Another blizzard? *What time was it now?* The dim light from the window did not produce enough light to see the clock on the piano.

Soldiers would probably come after twelve, or after one, two, three? I almost wished the arrest had been already made, my fate sealed.

The wind was getting stronger. It produced howling sounds. Through the window I could see snowflakes twirling around. The snow and my pressing worries put me in pensive mood. It brought to mind a favorite Russian poem.

The storm covers the sky with dark clouds
The wind twirls the falling snow
Sometimes the wind howls like a wild beast
Sometimes it cries like a child
Sometimes it whistles in the eaves of an old cottage
Sometimes it knocks on the window like a late traveler.

I always liked poetry. It was at times like this that its soothing qualities quieted my spirit. Pushkin was my favorite; he could do that. I especially loved *Eugene Onegin*. Tatiana, the heroine, was my role model. She probably was a favorite for every young Russian girl.

Sadly I told myself, "Lara, you will never have a chance to love, there is only horror ahead of you." Suddenly my thoughts were interrupted by a noise. There was a knock on the window. I jumped from my bed. My heart was racing. I could feel every beat in my throat. Silently I went to the window and looked out. There was nobody there, just wind and snow.

Still I stood listening—nothing unusual. I crawled back into bed and pulled the blankets to my chin. I was shivering. *Oh, God, how many more hours to wait?* In order not to think, I started to recite Tatiana's famous love letter. I knew it by heart. It was a long poem and I whispered the stanzas until, finally, my memory failed me. I could not go on. Exhausted, I fell asleep. When I opened my eyes I had to squint. The room was full of sunshine. Sun rays coming through the window, glittering on the fresh-fallen snow, were especially bright.

Papa was feeding wood into the stove. Mama was mending something.

"What time is it?" I asked. Mama looked at me. "You slept quite well, Lara. It is past nine o'clock." I sat up in bed understanding I was still at home. The day passed quickly. It was Sunday. I helped with house chores and did my homework. In the afternoon I went for a walk with mama.

That night I slept off and on, still listening, but when morning came I knew Olga kept everything I said to herself. Despite her communistic upbringing she was a good person. I felt admiration and respect for her. *The system cannot corrupt everyone,* I thought. As I got ready for school, I almost missed the train, for I had tried to delay facing Olga.

When the train arrived in the city I watched her disembark and stayed behind. She walked to school with her head bent down, her scarf covering the lower part of her face.

The morning was gray and cold. The sun too hid its face behind the clouds. At school, I think both of us tried to avoid each other. I felt I was the guilty one as Olga's troubled face rose before my eyes.

The week passed without incident. I saw Grisha in the company of Martha several times, but we did not speak. One week was left until winter vacation, then Misha would return. I needed to talk to him, to tell him everything.

On the last day of school when I got off the train on the way home, Olga happened to be right in front of me. I followed for quite a while and then, without thinking, caught up with her and touched her elbow. She stopped and turned to face me. There was a surprised sparkle in her eyes. "Lara?"

"Olga," I said, almost whispering, "Can you forgive me?"

"Forgive what?"

"I shouldn't have told you what I did last time we talked."

Olga shrugged her shoulders and said calmly, "I pressed you with questions." She hesitated for a moment and then added, "Did you really think I could report you? Do you know that your words *Do your duty, Olga,* still ring in my ears? But, oh, Lara, how could I take that upon my conscience...?" Her voice choked up.

"Olga," I started saying, but she put her hand up.

"I haven't finish yet." She took a breath and continued. "I want to explain to you, that what you told me made no difference in my beliefs. I still think the old world had to be changed, and when trees are cut splinters fly." She looked at me. "I'm so sorry, Lara, for your misfortunes, but the future will show us who is right."

I felt relieved. I did not harm this innocent girl. "Thank you for sparing me, Olga."

A smile lighted her face. "I like you very much, you silly girl with big sad eyes."

Impulsively, I came close and embraced her tightly. "Oh, Olga." That was all I could say.

She returned my embrace, and we stood for a while holding each other. A girl from the East, a girl from the West...

Letting her go I said, "You must understand now why I was pulling away from you. I think it would be wiser for us to be apart.

Olga nodded. "I agree, it will be better to do that." It was time to go. "Take care of yourself, Lara."

"God bless you, Olga," I whispered.

There was peace in my mind as I walked home. The ordeal was over, but I would never forget that terrible night when I was expecting the arrest. How lucky that I kept everything to myself and did not cause my parents undue worry. I could look forward to two great weeks of vacation. It would be lovely just to stay home.

29   A Sad Farewell

T he next day I sat down to write a letter to Tonia. I had almost forgotten about her. I was certain she was already married for several months, by now.

Tonia,
I got your letter two weeks ago. It was so painful to read it. My poor, dear friend, and you are so far away, I cannot help you. We are still alive and together. We live now in this small community—I commute to school. We have one room, but it is warm, and we have enough to eat.
I see Grisha at school every day, but we talk to each other very rarely. He took the news of your marriage very hard. I'm worried about him. I never know what will happen tomorrow. I hope your life will be bearable. Please write.
I love you very much,
Lara

On the second day of my winter break, early in the afternoon, there was a knock on the door. Cautiously, I opened it.

"Misha!" I exclaimed. I was so glad to see him.

He was dressed in a warm, tan coat, fur hat and knit gloves. Stepping into the room, he took off the hat, and showing it to us said with a kind of embarrassment, "This is my newest acquisition. Now I look like a Soviet." In our small room, crowded with furniture Misha looked awfully big.

"So lovely to see you," mother said with a smile. "Take off your coat and sit down—here, right at the table and have some tea with us."

"Chamomile tea," I added. "Remember how many flowers we picked last summer?"

Clumsily he removed his gloves and coat. Sitting down, he looked questionably at me. He sensed that I was observing him. "Do I look all right?" He asked.

"You gained some weight," I stated hesitantly and instantly regretted my remark.

Misha felt uneasy. "You see, my food in college is mostly bread, potatoes and milk. Meat is scarce and so are vegetables, and I'm a big boy and always hungry," he smiled embarrassingly.

"Misha, Misha, I'm so sorry, I shouldn't have said that." I tried to apologize.

"No, no, that's all right. Anyway, that's the truth, and I know I look bad, especially with my shaven head, but in the dormitory it's so easy to get lice." His eyes looked sadly at me. I felt even worse.

Pouring the tea into his cup, I said warmly, "My dear friend, to me you look like good old Misha."

After the tea we went for a walk. We had much to talk about. The day was not very cold—clouds but no snow. It was slippery. "Hold my arm," Misha said. I slid my hand over his sleeve. Then I started telling him about Olga—about our conversation on the train, about my outburst.

"Oh, Lara, Lara, how could you? I told you to be careful, careful!"

"I know, I know, but at that time I could not be silent, even when I was sure that Olga would report me to the police. Oh, Misha, those two nights when I expected an arrest, I will never forget them."

"But you are here, you are all right!"

"Yes, I wasn't arrested. Later I talked to Olga. She said she simply could not report me, could not have my life on her conscience."

"You see," Misha stopped walking and turned to face me. "You see, there is one sign that Russia is not dead yet. A new generation is growing up with morals that even communist teaching can't corrupt." There was a glow in his eyes. "As I told you before, we just need time. Stalin will not live forever."

"Is that what you believe, Misha? Wait and do nothing?"

"Yes, I do, and you know, I think it's good that you had that talk with Olga. You planted a seed of truth in her mind. Of course, she is still full of propaganda, but that seed of doubt will grow."

"It's dangerous for her," I stated.

"Oh, Lara, sooner or later she will understand what communism really is. Thank God nothing bad happened to you," he added tenderly. "Now," he smiled, "to cheer you up, I'll tell you a joke I heard in college. You know that a communist Russian is called red and a democratic Russian is called white. Anyway, when a Russian is born, he is white. At school, with propaganda, he becomes pink, by the time he is in college he is bright red, but when he enters the work force the color starts fading. When a Russian dies in a concentration camp or in prison, he is pure white."

"It is a good joke," I laughed.

Misha continued, "At college I'm in touch with many Russian young men. I can't say much, but I can observe. It's a new generation, unspoiled, used to a hard life, eager to learn."

I listened silently, thinking about Grisha. How different they both were, I thought, weighing Misha's patience against Grisha's actions. "How long will it take for this sickness to pass?" I asked gloomily.

He shrugged his shoulders. "This, I don't know."

"Grisha doesn't want to wait," I whispered.

"What do you mean?"

I told him about my suspicions, about the underground organizations, about Martha. "Stupid, how can they be so stupid! What will they achieve by being dead or in a concentration camp?" Misha almost shouted.

I did not want to contradict him, but in my mind, I agreed with Grisha.

New Year was approaching, 1941. What would it bring?

So many things had happened in the last twelve months. On New Year's Eve my parents and I went to bed early. Lying in bed I was thinking about my past New Year's Eves. Tonia was with me and I was still in my own home. I felt so sad. *Oh, Lara, stop it, go to sleep*, I reprimanded myself.

The next day Misha came about one o'clock in the afternoon. He brought a pine tree planted in a pot.

"I planted it last fall, Lara, and thought that if it would grow, I would bring it for you on your birthday. Anyway, I am wishing you a happy birthday," he said softly, looking into my eyes.

"How lovely, Misha. Thank you so much. You know it will be my Christmas tree. Last year I didn't have one." Misha also brought me a little book of poetry by Lermontov, a contemporary of Pushkin.

The day was so cold that we did not dare go for a walk. It felt as if the air itself had turned into tiny icicles, that pierced the lungs while breathing.

We read some poetry, shared a meal and played cards. It was warm in the room, the stove filled to capacity. Wood burned with a crackling sound. The turbulent world was somewhere behind the walls of our room, but here the four of us enjoyed tranquility and peace, even some laughter. It was growing dark. Misha had to catch the train back to the city. He was saying good-bye when someone knocked on the window. I looked out and saw a figure of a man, all bundled up. Misha went to let him in. When the man took off his hat and scarf we were all surprised to see Grisha. "My God," I exclaimed astonished. "It's Grisha!"

"Greetings to everybody and happy birthday, Lara," he said in a hoarse voice. "It's really cold out here." He looked at me with embarrassment. I knew something important had brought him.

"Come in, come in." Mama was already pouring some hot tea. "We must warm you up."

Without taking off his coat, he nervously accepted the cup. Holding it with both hands he sipped the steaming liquid slowly. For a while there was silence. I could feel the tension mounting. "Grisha," I said, "what happened? What's wrong?" He put the cup on the table and moved closer to me.

"Lara, I came to talk to you. I have to talk to you. It's urgent and very important." He looked around and said apologetically, "I have to talk to Lara alone."

"Do you expect the rest of us to step outside?" Misha's voice was full of sarcasm, and his face, usually kind, was hardened.

"You can trust all of us. You can speak here openly." Mother assured him.

Grisha shook his head. "It's impossible, I have to talk only to Lara, alone. I wish I didn't have to, but I must."

"I will go outside with you, Grisha."

"Please, Lara, it will be only for a short moment."

I reached for my coat, but Misha's hand grabbed my wrist. "You will not go outside, it is too cold." The grip of his hand was almost painful.

"Misha..., let go of my hand. Don't you see I have to talk to Grisha?"

"No. If he has anything to say, he can say it here. I won't let you go outside." I looked at Misha in surprise. I had never seen him like this, but I was getting angry. I jerked my hand out of his grip and put on my coat. Mother handed me my hat and scarf.

"I feel that Grisha really has to talk to Lara," she spoke with a hesitant tone.

"I am sorry for all the commotion I've caused. Please forgive me." He waved his hand for a good-bye and added, "I will wait for you outside, Lara."

I was about to follow him, but Misha stopped me. "Boots. You forgot to put on your boots."

Outside I almost choked with the first breath of air. Grisha was waiting for me a few yards away. When I came close he said, "Our organization sprang a leak our leader was arrested a couple of days ago, together with a few others. More arrests will follow." He paused for a second and then continued, "I can be arrested any time."

I listened, horrified. *Oh, my God.* "But you are still free! You must run away, hide immediately."

He shrugged his shoulders. "Where will I go? And, anyway, I'm not running," he said proudly. "Now, listen, I have a big favor to ask of you. My aunt, you know her, she'll be devastated when they take me. Help her, please. I know I should probably not ask you this, but she has no one except me, and she likes you and..."

"Of course, I will do anything to help her," I interrupted. "I can visit her almost every day after school. But you, Grisha, you, I don't want to lose you. I can't lose you." I couldn't accept the thought of not ever seeing him again.

"Never mind me," he said dryly. "And what I told you about the arrest is only for your ears, remember that."

"That's understandable," I replied, my voice cracking.

"I have to go," he said and turned away from me and started walking.

"Grisha, no." I shouted. "Wait!" I ran up to him. He stopped. I hesitated for a second then put my arms around his neck and hugged him. A few moments passed then, gently, he put my arms down.

"Stay safe, dear girl," he whispered and disappeared into the darkness.

I turned to go home. A tall figure blocked my path. "Misha."

"I saw you run to him and embrace him. Does he mean that much to you? What did he want from you?" I heard an icy voice.

"I can't tell you that."

"You used to be open with me, Lara."

I did not answer.

"Oh, Lara, Lara, what did you get yourself into?"

I lifted my face to Misha. "Grisha made me promise not to tell anyone. Please understand."

"But I'm worried about you. Please let me help," he begged.

"I have to deal with this myself," I said firmly.

"You won't change your mind?"

"No, I cannot."

"Then it's obvious you don't need me," Misha said bitterly. Turning he added, "you would never run to me and embrace me like you did Grisha."

"I'm so sorry," was all I could say.

"Go home, it's cold," he said flatly and walked away.

I realized I had lost them both.

Back in the room I explained to my parents that I could not reveal what Grisha told me. They accepted and understood. Why couldn't Misha?

For the next few days the possibility of Grisha's arrest haunted me. School started on January sixth. That was Christmas Eve according to the Russian Orthodox Church calendar. I decorated the little pine tree that Misha had given me with white cotton balls.

On the first day of school I searched for Grisha. I saw him from afar. I was happy. Martha was also in my class, so maybe... *Oh, dear God, please spare them both*, I prayed.

Occasionally I shared a few words with Olga. She was friendly and seemed to be happy. Misha left for college without saying good-bye. He probably would not write to me anymore. Sad, but what could I do?

Life again fell into a routine—school, homework, and piano lessons.

30   TATIANA NIKOLAIEVNA

Around the middle of January when I came home from school, I found a visitor in our room, a tall, stately woman, probably in her late thirties. A thick braid of light-blond hair adorned her pretty head.

"I am Tatiana Nikolaievna," she said extending her hand, "and you are Lara the pianist." Gray eyes looked at me in a friendly manner. "I heard you play last night when I walked by your lodging. You play very well."

"Thank you," I mumbled, taking off my overcoat and boots. "I'm pleased to meet you," I added.

"Tatiana is a singer from St. Petersburg, that is Leningrad," mother corrected herself quickly. "She wants you to accompany her singing."

"Yes, Lara, please can you help me? My family and I came here a couple months ago. This is such a small community, I was afraid I would not be able to find an accompanist."

"But I'm only a piano student and very busy with schoolwork," I replied, reluctant to accept her offer.

"Let us try. Give me just a few hours of your time, maybe next Sunday morning. Please," Tatiana was insisting.

"Lara, it could be a good experience for you," mother added.

So we agreed to meet at her place on Sunday at nine o'clock. Tatiana gave us her address and left.

Father was shaking his head. "Do you know what place that is?" He asked. "It's Prince Radziwill's hunting lodge, very beautiful. The woman's husband must be an important communist if they were assigned to live there."

Already I regretted that I had accepted the offer. I remembered Prince Radziwill. He came a couple of times to our house. Father was conducting his business. The prince and his wife, an Italian princess, had a baby girl. During the summer months, the family lived in a remodeled part of the castle. Their main residence was in Warsaw. Once, while on a business trip, father took me to the castle. I remembered their huge, beautiful lawns full of flowers. I was eager only to see the hunting lodge.

Sunday was cold but sunny. Several inches of snow had fallen during the night, and covered the already icy road. Walking was hard.

A path led me through the woods into a clearing. In the middle of it stood the hunting lodge. I stopped for a while admiring the impressive structure, built probably two hundred years ago. It was constructed from big brown logs, two stories high. Several inches of snow covered the slanted roof. The glass panels of the windows reflected the surrounding pine trees. Icicles hanging from the eaves sparkled in the sun. I breathed, *Oh, God, how beautiful and peaceful it is.* A few steps led to the porch and a massive oak door. I knocked. In a while, a young peasant girl opened the door and let me in.

Stepping into a big hall one had to look up at the high ceiling. Winding steps led to a balcony on the second floor.

"Wait here," the girl mumbled and disappeared into an adjoining room. I let my curiosity guide my eyes. Large chunks of wood crackled in a huge fireplace that gave out a pleasant warmth. *It was probably like this in olden times when Radziwill had hunting parties,* I said under my breath. Several old portraits of men in Polish hunting costumes appeared to stare gloomingly at me, as if to say, *What are you doing here, girl?* I had an eerie feeling of stepping back into the past.

"There you are, Lara," Tatiana's booming voice seemed to fill the hall. "Come in, we're having breakfast. Please join us." She shook my hand and added, "I am glad you came."

I followed her into the next room, which happened to be a dining room. The long oak table could probably seat more than twenty people. At one end, food was served. Tatiana Nikolaievna introduced me to her husband, a tall heavy-set man with short, grayish hair, who just nodded at me.

"And here, Lara, is our son, Boria." She stood close to a pale, skinny little boy, maybe six or seven years of age, and stroked his blond hair. The boy's light-blue eyes looked questionably at me.

"Boria," his mother continued, "has been very ill with pneumonia. He's better now and has to build up his strength, but he refuses to eat. I don't really know what to do." There was desperation in her voice.

I sat down on the chair next to the boy. The girl who opened the front door for me, brought me a cup of tea. I thanked her, saying, "Just the tea, please. I already had breakfast."

I noticed two sunny-side-up eggs on the plate in front of the boy, a buttered roll and a cup of chocolate. The food was untouched. Looking at me seriously, Boria asked, "Did you come to play with me? I have so many toys but nobody wants to play with me," he said wistfully. I felt instant sympathy for the little fellow.

"All right," I smiled, "after you finish your breakfast, I would love to see all your toys."

He shook his head stubbornly. "I don't like to eat, and I hate eggs."

I noticed a small jar of mustard on the table. "You know what, Boria," I said, "maybe if I put a little mustard over your eggs they will taste better. When I was a little girl, an egg with mustard was my favorite food."

"You liked eggs with mustard?"

"Yes, I did, very much. You want to try?"

Boria shrugged his shoulders. The blue eyes watched me smear the mustard over the food.

"Now, open your mouth and I want to see if you can eat just three spoonfuls."

Obediently the boy opened his mouth and I fed him three spoonfuls.

"More," he said swallowing the food, "and more mustard." Soon the plate was empty. The parents watched us breathlessly.

"Very good, Boria," I said cheerfully, "and now the roll and the chocolate."

"Oh, no," he said.

"Oh, yes," I insisted, "roll and chocolate."

"Then you'll play with me?"

"I promised I would and I will," I assured the boy.

So the roll and hot chocolate were soon gone.

"I'm stuffed," Boria sighed, patting his stomach.

I turned to Tatiana. "Can we have our session later? I promised Boria to play with him."

She was all smiles. "But of course, of course. Oh, Lara, I am grateful to you for making him eat."

"Come on, come on," Boria grabbed my hand and pulled me toward the stairs. His room was big and sunny. There really were many toys. Some were scattered all over the floor.

"Did you bring all of the toys from Leningrad?" I could not help myself asking.

"No, I got all these toys from my uncle, and he even promised me to bring some more," Boria said and whispered confidently, "My uncle is a very important communist."

A chill went through me. The toys probably belonged to the children of deported families. I had an urge to immediately leave his room and this house, but Boria's eyes looked innocently at me. I forced myself to stay and play with the child.

Later, I had a session with his mother. She had a beautiful voice, and I enjoyed accompanying her. We agreed that I would come next Sunday. Boria followed me to the door.

"We will play again, yes?" He asked. I hesitated. "Oh, please, please?"

"You know what, Boria? I'll play with you under one condition," I said, "that for the whole week you'll eat well."

"I promise I will, I will, just come."

I smiled and patted him on the head.

I walked slowly home, breathing the frosty air with pleasure. I was thinking about the little boy. Obviously he was lonely, with no playmates. Local children did not associate with Soviet children. The communists had brought so much suffering to the population. I myself hated them intensely. Then why did I agree to come again next Sunday? The last thing I wanted was the company of Soviet followers. But Boria was sickly and pale. He promised me he would eat well. How could I disappoint him?

The following Sunday, I went to the lodge again. Boria opened the door himself before I had a chance to knock.

"I knew you would come, I knew," he shouted happily, "and I ate and ate, ask mama."

Tatiana Nikolaievna was standing behind the boy. "Look, Lara, how well Boria looks already." She was radiant.

Of course we first went to the playroom. That morning I learned that the boy's uncle who was supplying him with toys was the head of the NKVD in my hometown. It was hard for me to touch the toys; it felt as if there were blood on them. *My God, what am I doing here?* I asked myself, but innocent blue eyes looked at me with such contentment and happiness that I was compelled to stay.

How am I going to get out of this? I was thinking later when Tatiana announced her decision to give her own concert in a few months. After that, I had no choice but to commit myself to coming every Sunday to the lodge.

I thought about my dilemma a great deal. It brought a heavy weight to my stomach. Music and war, what strange partners. I was torn between the happy thought of playing for a concert and having to consort with Soviet sympathizers. And then there was school and Grisha. If only he would talk to me. It was already the first week of February. The weather was blizzard-like. It was a struggle to get to the railroad station and to walk to school. Each time I saw Grisha I tried to catch his glance, but most of the time he turned his face away.

All right, Grisha, the most important thing for me is that you are still free and I can see you, I told him silently.

31   THE ARREST

One day a letter came from Tonia. I opened it with trembling hands. It was dated three weeks earlier.

My dearest friend, Lara!
I got your letter. I was so glad to hear from you. I've been married now for a few months. We live in this village with my husband's parents. They're good to me. My brother Andrei attends school. He's gained weight. He always laughs when his belly is full; he was awful hungry before. Mother passed away a month ago. It's a big loss for me. She died in peace. We took good care of her to the end, my husband and I. He's a good man and loves me very much. I don't know what's happening, but I think I'm falling in love with my own husband, my Knight? Don't laugh, Lara, but he even has a horse, not white, but brown, and he rides it splendidly. I'm all right and almost happy, and one more thing, I'm pregnant. I learned it recently. Can you imagine that I'm going to have a little baby?
Don't worry about me, and please write to me as soon as you get this letter. I love you as always.
Tonia

I folded the letter and put it back into the envelope. The address was the same, only Tonia's name had changed.

God's ways are unpredictable, I assured myself.

It was such a relief to know that my dear friend was well and even happy, such a change from the awful circumstance that consumed her existence before, almost unbelievable. I was happy, real glad.

I opened the letter and read it again slowly. Some strange emotions were stirring inside me. I suddenly felt as if I had lost a friend. For years Tonia was part of my life, even when she was far away. Now she moved in a different dimension. She had a husband, and was going to have a child. I shook my head, Tonia with a baby. I did not have to worry about her anymore. This was good, only why did I feel such emptiness, even sadness? *I realized painfully, Tonia has her own life now, she doesn't need me.*

Grisha, too, did not want to be part of my life. Even Misha had stopped writing to me. I felt as if all my friends had deserted me. Tears misted my eyes.

Oh, Lara, Lara, stop being sorry for yourself, just remember how you felt those two nights when you were expecting an arrest, I tried to comfort myself.

Unexpectedly, by the end of February there was a warming spell. The temperature rose from away below zero to almost past freezing point. March was around the corner with its promise of spring. The last day of February was upon us. As usual I got off the train and began walking toward school. Vasia appeared in front of me. One look at his face and fear choked my throat.

"Vasia, what has happened?"

"Let's get away from the crowd," he said, leading me to the side.

I stopped, and facing him, exclaimed, "Tell me now."

Vasia tried to avoid my stare. "I have bad news. Grisha was arrested last night, his aunt came over to our house at six o'clock in the morning." He said all this in one breath and with a flat ring of finality.

Slowly I filled my lungs to capacity. My whole body suddenly felt weak. I had lived with the possibility of Grisha's arrest for quite some time. Still the blow was hard. Vasia took my hand. "Come, we can't just stand here, let's walk." I followed him mutely. For the first time I felt a dense and complete hopelessness. We walked in silence.

"Lara, say something."

I heard Vasia's voice as if from afar. I shrugged my shoulders thinking, what is there to say? Grisha is arrested, interrogated, tortured probably, and how am I going to handle this hurt?

Finally I heard my voice ask, "Is Grisha's aunt at your house now? I have to see her, I promised Grisha to help her. Can we go to your house now, Vasia?"

"No, not now. Now you have to go to school and then you can come, I mean after school." Vasia's voice was stern.

"I don't want to go to school," I retorted angrily. "What for? Anyway, I can't take this life anymore." We stopped not far from the school entrance. "Vasia," I looked at him pleadingly, "I don't think I can face my classmates. I don't think I can go on."

"Hey, don't fall apart, Lara, and don't look at me with those tragic green eyes." Vasia moved closer to me and was almost whispering in my ear. "You're going to go on like all the people in the Soviet Union do." He took a breath before he continued. "Listen, Lenin killed thousands of people. Stalin is killing thousands more. The country is mad with a madman on top, and how long all of this will last, God only knows."

Vasia stopped and looking suspiciously around added, "It's wrong of me to tell you all this, but I want you to understand you're not the only one suffering, millions are." He touched my cheek with his fingers, "Now, go."

"Wait, Vasia." I grabbed his arm. "Wait, I have to show you something." I reached into my purse and got out Tonia's letter, which I carried with me. "Read it. It's from Tonia."

"From Tonia?" Carefully he unfolded the paper and started reading. After a while Vasia's face lit up. Smiling he returned the letter. "Unbelievable, is it not?" He shook his head. "From complete despair to happiness. I'm delighted for Tonia. And you see, Lara, one never knows what the future holds for us."

Reluctantly I entered the school building. It was unusually quiet in my classroom. I looked for Martha, she was absent. So was her constant friend, Valia. *Martha is probably arrested, too.* I surmised.

During recess, students whispered to each other about the arrests of their friends. I could not concentrate on anything, wanting the classes to be over. There was a pain in the pit of my stomach.

Finally the last bell rang. I rushed outside, but was interrupted by Olga. "Lara, wait, I have to talk to you."

Without a word I brushed her aside.

"Lara, please."

Vasia was waiting outside.

"Let's go, Vasia, I have very little time before the train."

Vasia grabbed my hand. "Wait, Grisha's aunt went back to her house. She's expecting you there."

"Oh, no," I exclaimed, "it's much further than your place. I'll miss the train." I noticed that Olga stood next to us, listening.

"Olga, please leave us alone," I said angrily.

"I will not," she retorted. "Listen, Lara, go and visit Grisha's aunt and take the next train. I'll stop at your parents and explain everything. Grisha was in my class, I know what happened to him."

I hesitated for a moment. "You'll tell my parents I'll be on the next train?"

"I told you that already."

I turned to Vasia. "Vasia, this is Olga..."

"Go, you'll be late," he interrupted. "We will get acquainted by ourselves if Olga will let me walk her to the station, of course."

I heard Olga laugh.

"I don't mind at all," she said warmly.

I walked with a heavy heart. How could I help Grisha's dear, old aunt? Last year her sister and her family were transported to Siberia. Grisha was all she had. Would it have been better if Grisha were deported with his parents last year?

I came to the little house and knocked at the door. There was no answer. I pushed on the door. It opened. The day was gray, the small windows did not let in much light. In a corner, in a big stuffed chair sat Grisha's aunt Nina. I stopped and observed her for a second. As usual, she was immaculately dressed. Black skirt and white blouse. An old-fashioned brooch adorned the collar. Her gray hair was pinned in a bun on top of her head.

She stared dead ahead, not noticing me. I approached and said her name quietly, "Nina Aleksandrovna." She focused her eyes on me and a faint smile appeared on her lips.

"Lara, dear girl, come in, come in." She made an effort to stand up. In a few steps I was by her chair, knelt and buried my face in her skirt.

I wanted to cry but knew I had to hold my tears. "I'm sorry." That was all I could say. She stroked my hair. The gentle movement of her hand was pleasant and calming. "What are we going to do?" I mumbled. She lifted my face to hers. Her lips trembled when she said, "We can pray, that is all we can do."

Clumsily I got up from my knees. "Can I help with anything?" I asked.

"Some tea would be good," she said quietly. I left her and went to the kitchen. Soon the water was boiling. I found some bread and jam in the cupboard. I had to make the old lady eat something. We sat down at the table. It was hard for both of us to start talking about Grisha. Finally I asked, "Are you going to the NKVD to learn something?"

"What for? They won't tell me anything. Vasia said many young people were arrested. There will be no trials, no court procedures. They'll all be sent to labor camps and that is that." I heard anger in Nina's voice.

"It is hard for me to think that Grisha'll be in a labor camp," I whispered. "I liked him very much."

"I know, I know, my dear girl. I am heartily sorry for you, for all the people caught in this craziness. This is such unbelievable madness caused by ruthless fanatics."

"And there's nothing we can do about it. Grisha tried and..." I could not continue.

There was a pause, then Nina said, "You know what, Lara, when I look back I think how good life was under the Tzar. It was not perfect. Lots of improvement had to be done, but we had freedom, we had dignity, we had self-respect."

I sensed that she needed to talk, so I asked about her previous life. She was eager to do that and I listened attentively.

Soon I had to leave to catch my train. I promised Nina I would visit her as often as possible.

"Never mind me," she said faintly. My life is over. I worry about you."

I embraced her tightly.

When I arrived home I was surprised to see Vasia. He and papa were talking in low voices.

"How is Grisha's aunt Nina?" Mama asked.

"She tried to be calm, but I know Grisha's arrest hit her hard." I turned to Vasia, "What an unexpected visit."

"Well, as you know I followed Olga to the train station and, as we did not finish our conversation, I decided to ride with her on the train."

"The conversation must have been extremely interesting," I teased.

"Olga is a lovely girl," Vasia said with some embarrassment, "and I haven't talked to your father in quite a long time. Any objections?"

"Oh, Vasia, I am glad you are here." I patted him on the shoulder.

"Vasia has some rather fresh information for me about the political situation," papa said.

I was anxious to hear all about it, so after Vasia left I had a long talk with my father. He came to the conclusion that war was absolutely unavoidable. The question was who would start first, Hitler or Stalin?

It appeared that Stalin was waiting for Hitler to invade England and as the Germans would be entangled in this operation, Stalin could then hit Hitler in the back with all his might. And *might* he had. Stalin was obsessed with the idea of global revolution. Since he came to power he began militarizing the country with complete disregard for human life or human needs.

His immediate goal was to invade Europe and to start a communist revolution in every country that his soldiers occupied.

"But Hitler is not stupid," papa said. "In my opinion he is only pretending to invade England in order not to provoke Stalin. I'm sure he's already transferring his main force to the Eastern front, waiting for the right time to attack."

"When will be the right time, papa?" I asked.

"May, June, not later than that," was his answer.

May or June were still some weeks away. By that time Grisha would have been transported to a concentration camp in Siberia, I thought sadly. Still there was hope that with war, communism might collapse.

Spring was in the air. The weather was warm, pleasant. Puddles, formed from melting snow, reflected blue skies and sunshine. Pine trees were losing their snow covers.

I had to answer Tonia's letter. Knowing that she was all right, and maybe even happy, evoked a peaceful feeling in me. I began the letter.

My dearest friend, Tonia,

Thank you for your letter. It is still hard for me to comprehend that you are married, and expecting a baby, but, oh how happy I am for you. Miraculously you survived last year's ordeal. Makes one think how unpredictable fate is. I'm so sorry about the death of your mother.

Tonia dear, I can still hardly believe that you are going to have a child. I think it's wonderful. God bless you all.

Now about me? We are still in the same small village in the woods. I commute to school. In a few months I will graduate. What lies ahead for me, I don't know, I can't make any plans. I'm not allowed to go to

*college. To be honest Tonia, I'm slowly losing the
will to live. Forgive me for writing these sad words.
I embrace you with all my love.
Lara*

I did not write to her about Grisha. Why make
her any more unhappy?

March was passing by. I was very busy. Tatiana
Nikolaievna was planning her concert in April. In
order to add variety to the program, she wanted me
to play several piano solos. I chose a few pieces from
Seasons, Tchaikovsky's delightful compositions for
each month of the year.

There was a great deal of rehearsing to do with
Tatiana Nikolaievna. Boria was getting more and
more attached to me. When I approached the lodge
I always saw his little, round face behind the glass
panel of the downstairs window. Then he would run
to me, grab my hand, and I had to play with him for
hours.

Sometimes he would stick his stomach out, pat it
and say, "Look I'm getting fat. You should see how
much I ate today." I found, despite everything, I liked
the little boy very much.

In the meantime, a romance was developing
between Vasia and Olga. Almost every morning
Vasia would wait for Olga at the railroad station and
walk her to school. There was a glow on Olga's face
and an embarrassed smile on her lips. Vasia seemed
to lose his happy-go-lucky disposition. Some
seriousness appeared on his face. Two young people

were reaching out to each other. *Well,* I thought, *love can develop even under hard conditions of life.*

On the other hand I felt lonelier than ever. I missed Grisha. I did not have much contact with him before his arrest, but at least I saw him every school day.

It was unbearable to think what he might be enduring now. Was he alive, still in prison, or already in a labor camp?

And Misha had not written a single letter since he left for college in January. We had been such good friends. I could talk to him about anything, confide in him. He told me he had feelings for me. I knew he was jealous of Grisha. His pride was hurt when he saw me in Grisha's arms. What a big word, pride. He did not even want to know how I was doing.

Now I needed him so much. I needed a friendly soul to care for me. Often I had an urge to stop at Misha's parents house and ask how he was doing, but I did not. I, too, had pride. March was coming to an end.

32   ABDUCTION TO *NKVD*

On April first, after I came home from school, I had to rush to rehearse with Tatiana Nikolaievna. In two weeks the whole program should be ready.

"When are you going to be home?" Father asked.

"I don't know exactly, maybe after five. I'll fix supper tonight, papa. Do we have any rice?"

"I'll look, just wait a second. Yes, we do," he said getting a jar from the cupboard.

"Can you cook rice so it will be done by five-thirty?" I asked.

Twice a week mother taught Russian to the railroad workers until eight o'clock. On those days it was my turn to prepare supper.

The rehearsal went very well.

"One or two minor details and we'll be ready," Tatiana Nikolaievna told me. And added, "Oh, Lara,

I don't know how to thank you for everything, for helping me and Boria. I believe you saved his life."

Boria tugged at my shirt and said, "After this concert you'll still come and play with me? Won't you?" There was anxiety in his voice.

"Of course she will," Tatiana Nikolaievna answered for me. "We'll plan another concert, Lara?"

"We'll see," I answered hesitantly. The clock showed a few minutes past five. I felt extremely tired. It was time to go home.

When I approached our lodgings I saw father standing in the frame of the open door. One look at his face and I knew something was wrong.

"What's the matter?" I asked, coming closer.

"Lara, ten minutes ago two men came here and wanted to talk to you." His voice was tense.

"What kind of men?" I asked. "NKVD?"

"I don't know, but obviously Soviet men, not in uniform, though. They wanted you to go to the Militia as soon as you come home."

Militia? I thought. Why? Militia was the Soviet police, usually not connected with political matters.

"Did they say anything else, papa?"

"No, only for you to hurry."

We were looking at each other anxiously. Papa made one step towards me.

"I'm scared, girlie, so scared," he said in a trembling voice.

"So am I," I whispered and added as I started to leave. "I better go, I don't know what this is all about, but I must report to them."

"Lara, wait," father shouted, "Wait, don't go."

I turned to look at him. Oh, God, there was such tension and pain in his face. His right hand was stretched out toward me as if he wanted to stop me.

"Papa, it's all right. I'll be back soon." Tears filled my eyes. "I love you, papa. I love you very much."

At this moment I realized how dear my father was to me but I must continue on my way. I knew where the Militia was located. The building was on the outskirts of the village, surrounded by trees. *I'll take a shortcut across the railroad tracks*, I said to myself. I did not want to speculate why I was summoned. It was better to get there quickly and find out.

Soon I was approaching the building. The place seemed to be deserted. No lights in the windows. It was already dusk.

I went up a couple of steps and knocked on the door. Silence.

I knocked harder—nothing. An uneasy feeling overwhelmed me.

God, what am I going to do? Stay here longer or go home? My head was full of questions.

Undecided, I lingered. I realized rather sadly, that the fear of disobeying was already implanted in me. I knocked again, knowing that no one was inside.

The wind picked up. The tops of the pine trees started to sing their monotonous song. I shivered. It was getting cold.

In a while I noticed two men emerging from the woods. I observed them as they approached. One was young looking, of medium height, the other, taller and much older. They wore knee-high, black leather boots and typical Soviet, cotton-stuffed, tan-colored half-coats. Flat caps covered their heads. Both men stopped in front of the porch on which I was standing.

"Larisa?" The older asked.

I nodded. Somehow I could not squeeze the words out through my tight throat.

"We thought we would intercept you on the road."

Not understanding what they wanted from me, I went down the steps.

"I was told to come to the Militia, but nobody's here," I said faintly.

"Never mind the Militia," the younger ordered. "Come, follow us."

He had a simple, round, peasant face. I was becoming frightened, but summoned my strength.

"Why follow you, and where to?" I asked defiantly. "And, besides, who are you? I was told to report to the Militia. The doors are closed and I'm going home."

Anger flushed the older man's face. "Stupid, stupid girl, better do what you are told," he almost shouted and pushed me towards the woods.

The younger one moved closer to me. "Are you going with us peacefully or do we have to drag you?"

I realized that resistance was impossible. Even if I shouted, no one would hear me. A thought, like lightning, flashed through my mind. *They will take me to the woods and attack me.*

Paralyzed with fear, I started walking, one man on my right, one on my left. I felt as if I was being escorted to the gallows.

Silently, we approached the woods. There was a dirt road I had not noticed before. We followed it. It was growing darker and darker. Suddenly I was almost blinded by a flood of lights. Squinting, I looked in the direction of the lights and saw a car on the left side of the road. There was a man behind the wheel. He must have switched on the headlights when he saw us. We reached the car. The older man opened the back door and told me to get in. Instinctively I hesitated.

"Oh, girl," there was annoyance in his voice, "get in and don't try anything."

I obeyed. Again there was one man on the right, one on the left of me. Were they afraid I would try to jump out?

"What took you so long?" Asked the driver.

"We had to wait for this silly girl," the younger replied. "Now, go, we've wasted enough time."

The car started rolling.

I was safe, I thought gratefully, *but where are we going?* In a few minutes we reached the highway leading to my hometown. My thoughts switched to my parents. *Papa, he was worried when I left. Possibly, after a while, he would decide to go to the Militia and find the building closed. What would he tell mama when she came home? Horrible, horrible suffering for them—not knowing what happened to me.*

I stirred. Turning to the younger man, I asked, "Please can you tell me where you're taking me?"

He shrugged his shoulders. "I'm not allowed to tell you that."

The older man turned his face toward me. It was a homely, narrow face with a crooked nose, broken in a fight, perhaps. "You'll find out soon enough," he said and I detected a sinister tone.

I could not give up questioning. "My parents don't know where I am, they'll be worried. I have to let them know when I'll be back."

The younger one laughed. "What a naive girl. You may never come back to your parents."

"Keep your mouth shut, Ivan," the other said.

It was useless to ask any more questions.

The car was speeding. I could faintly see the city lights on the horizon.

I knew for sure now that I was being arrested and the men were ordered to bring me to the NKVD. *What would happen to me?*

I remembered the horrors Natasha warned me about. *You have to face it, Lara, like Grisha, Martha, and many others have had to face it*, I thought. After a while a feeling of resignation gave me some peace.

Please, God, I prayed, *please help me, give me strength.*

We approached the suburbs of the city. Familiar landmarks passed by. Soon the car stopped at the gate of a massive, five-story building. I remembered it well from the cold night of father's arrest. It was the NKVD headquarters. There were lights in almost all of the front windows. Two soldiers standing in front of the gate opened it, let the car through and slammed it shut. A chill went through me. The car stopped at the back door of the building and my guards led me upstairs. In the stairway a solitary light bulb cast gloomy shadows.

On the second floor we entered a long corridor. There were several doors on one side. Benches lined the opposite wall with very few windows. Here, too, the hall was dimly lit by a single light bulb. Two uniformed soldiers stood at each end of the corridor.

"Sit and wait here," the older man said pointing to one of the benches.

Then both men talked shortly to one of the soldiers and left. I sat down and looked around. The walls of the corridor looked gray and cracked, and the dirty wooden floor had probably seen better days. There were four doors, each thickly padded, probably to muffle voices inside. Interrogating rooms? Torture rooms? The surroundings were so depressing, horror started to invade my mind as I envisioned the worst.

Oh, God, what will they do to me? I was cold and so alone. After a while, I stood up and approached one of the soldiers.

"Can you please show me where the rest room is?" I asked. He made a sign to follow him.

At the end of the hall was a narrow door.

"Here," the soldier said. "And be quick."

The rest room was small with no wash basin. The window, barred with two crisscrossed boards reminded me of the impossibility of escape. I went back to my bench. It was painful to think what my parents were going through by now, not knowing where I was.

"It is a nightmare, it is a nightmare," I said under my breath. My lips started to tremble and tears moistened my eyes.

Oh, no, Lara, no, I told myself. *Be strong. Keep your dignity. Don't show how frightened you are, and above all, don't cry.*

I closed my eyes and tried not to think. Instinctively, for self-preservation, I attempted to doze.

Time was passing. How much time? The sound of footsteps brought me out of semi-consciousness. A tall, slender man wearing a NKVD uniform and carrying a folder approached my bench and stopped a few feet in front of me. I stood up. He observed me for a few seconds, then opening the nearest door said, "I am Commissar Ipatov. Follow me."

I stepped into a middle-sized room. A large desk, standing close to a window, was the principle piece of furniture. There were several chairs around it. The commissioner sat behind the desk and switched on a lamp. The sudden glare on the desk seemed unusually bright, after spending so long in such a dark space.

Putting the folder on the desk and without looking at me, the commissar said, "Don't just stand there, close the door."

I obeyed and approached the desk.

Sitting across from me studying the folder, he gave another command, "Sit down."

These papers are about me, I thought. *Why so many? What kind of criminal am I?*

I observed Ipatov. Bald, with a long face, bushy, dark eyebrows and thin lips, he appeared to be in his fifties. On the wall behind the desk hung portraits of Lenin and Stalin. Their cold eyes seemed to regard me with malice. A Russian song came to my mind:

Oh, little bird,
you are caught in the net,
and you will never get away.

Suddenly my interrogator looked straight at me. The focus of his pale-blue eyes was so intense I cringed. A monotonous voice droned from the file as if it were a recitation:

"Larisa, age sixteen. Father, Vladimir, mother, Anastasia." He cleared his throat, and continued in the same dull voice.

"Deserted their country after the revolution and fled to Poland. Obviously, traitors and enemies of the Soviet Union."

He paused and looked at me with narrowed eyes. "Any brothers and sisters?"

I hesitated for a second and said, "No."

I did not want to reveal that my sister was in the German occupation zone. It was dangerous to have relatives in the West.

The man slammed his hand on the desk. "Liar! Liar!" He shouted. "We know you have a sister."

I tried to defend myself. "She doesn't live here. That's why I said no, I haven't seen her for two years."

"Don't you dare to lie when I ask you questions," he spat out through clenched teeth and added, "we know everything about you."

A sarcastic smile touched his lips.

"Now we will talk about your boyfriend, Grisha." I tensed.

"He is not my boyfriend, just a friend."

The man disregarded my remark.

"You know that he's arrested?"

"Yes, I understand that he's in prison."

"Do you know why?"

I shrugged my shoulders.

Suddenly the man started laughing. "Stupid, stupid kids. It's not only stupid, it's crazy."

He got up from the chair and began pacing the floor.

"A childish underground organization against the might of the Soviet people."

He laughed again, sounding like a harsh bark in the empty room.

"It's so ridiculous it's almost insane. Milk barely dry on their lips, yet these idiots want to play at conspiracy."

He jabbed a finger at me.

"The punishment will be severe. Very severe."

I listened painfully.

Abruptly he stopped in front of me. "Were you in this organization, too?"

"You said you knew everything about me, so you must know I was not," I answered bravely.

Anger flashed in the man's eyes.

"Don't get fresh with me," he snapped and resumed pacing.

My eyes followed him, noting his NKVD uniform — the brownish-green pants and shirt worn over the pants. His black leather belt had a strap across the chest. The high, black boots came up to his knees. He seemed to be deep in thought. Finally, approaching the desk he sat down. His piercing eyes focused on my face.

"You have to tell me everything you know about Grisha's activities."

"Grisha never confided in me."

"Do you think I'm so stupid as to believe that?" His voice rose in anger.

"Grisha saw you many times in the country, met you behind the music school building, at the railroad station and on New Year's Day he also came to see you."

I listened, startled, and realized that Grisha had been under surveillance all this time. I knew I would have to explain my friendship with Grisha, so I told him about Tonia, our childhood friendship, and about Tonia and Grisha's fondness for each other.

"They were close," I said.

The man listened silently. I continued.

"Grisha suffered very much when Tonia and her family were deported and when I received my first letter from Tonia I shared it with Grisha. We put together and mailed her a package with the things that she requested, that was my connection with Grisha," I concluded.

The commissar watched me closely as I spoke.

"Why did you meet secretly behind the railroad cars? Why not openly?" He asked.

"That was Grisha's idea. I had a feeling he didn't want to be seen with me."

"Why?"

I did not answer.

"I think you know why," he remarked coolly. He paused, shuffled some papers and spoke again. "Now one more question. When you saw Grisha last, what did you talk about?"

"He asked me to visit his aunt more often. She is old, lonely, and she likes me. I promised I would help."

"I believe you almost told the truth, and, yes, we know you do not belong to any underground organization."

I felt relieved. Hope appeared like a little sun ray. *Maybe they will let me go*, I thought.

"You know yourself that I did nothing wrong," I said firmly. "Please let me go home. My parents must be going out of their minds not knowing where I am."

My interrogator looked at me and even smiled.

"This will depend entirely on you."

My hope of release grew greater.

"Depend on me?" I repeated. "How?"

"Very simply," he said handing me a sheet.

"Just sign here and I personally will drive you home."

I took the paper and started reading it. It was a while before I understood the content. And then the earth seemed to break apart beneath my feet. I took a deep breath. *Oh, God, how could he, how could he even offer me something like this?* I thought.

The paper was a consent form committing me to collaborate with the NKVD. I was to become an informer, reporting anything I heard against the Soviet system and Joseph Stalin. I looked at the man with horror in my eyes. I could not believe he expected me to sign such a thing.

"Why are you looking at me like that?"

I did not utter a sound.

Ipatov lit a cigarette, took a couple of puffs and continued.

"You see, Lara, you can be very valuable to us. Nobody will suspect that you're working for the NKVD, so you can obtain important information from a number of sources. We need to know who else is in this stupid organization. You will contact people we suspect and encourage them to confide in you... of course, this will take some skill, but don't worry, we will teach you how to become an informer."

He spoke slowly looming over me as though to hypnotize me. Mutely, I watched him inhale the cigarette smoke then exhale in little ringlets, my eyes automatically following the circles. I felt as if something indescribably ugly had touched me. To spy on people. To be the cause of their arrest and possible death was absolutely unthinkable. I had one choice—to refuse no matter what the consequences. Sadly I understood that to do so was tantamount to pronouncing a death sentence or worse on my loved ones and myself. There was no other alternative. The paper was burning my hand. I put it down on the desk. The man handed me a pen.

"Here, Lara, sign it, and I will take you home."

I shook my head and tried to speak calmly.

"I can't. I can't collaborate with you."

"What?" The man raised his voice. "You stupid girl, don't play games with me. I don't have time for this nonsense. Do you know what will happen to you if you refuse? To you and to your parents?"

I took a deep breath.

"Yes, I know. But I can't. I can't have the lives of other people upon my conscience."

"Conscience!" The man shouted. "Conscience? For that word alone you deserve a concentration camp."

He rose from his chair and leaned over the desk. His stare was frightening.

"Sign," he commanded. "Sign right now!"

I, too, stood up, almost shouting, "Never! No matter what you do to me."

Hiding my fear, I looked straight into my tormentor's eyes. Rage twisted his face.

"You... you dare?"

He shook his fist.

For a moment we stood facing each other, then abruptly, shoving his chair back with such force that it fell with a crash, he left the room, slamming the door behind him.

I stood tense, motionless.

What now? What now? I asked myself. Seconds passed. Crazy thoughts passed through my mind. *Maybe I should try to escape. Run.* I moved cautiously toward the door, pausing before it, my heart pounding, then put my hand on the knob and tried to turn it. The door was locked.

That was a stupid idea anyway, I told myself. *How could you even think you could escape from here?*

I felt cold, frightened and very alone. Stiffly, I went to the corner of the room and sank to the floor. The walls seemed to shelter me. I pulled my knees to my chest and rested. My head felt heavy. Soon my thoughts scrambled and I drifted away in merciful sleep.

How long I slept, I don't know. I felt someone shaking my shoulder. I heard a voice saying, "Girl, girl, wake up."

"No, no," I mumbled resisting consciousness. Finally, I had to open my eyes. The voice belonged to a man who was bending over me.

"Get up," he said.

I scrambled to my feet and came face to face with a NKVD official. We stared at each other. Then strangely, the man smiled. It was a warm smile on a young, handsome face.

For a silent moment he observed me, then said, "poor girl, I know you are scared, but maybe I can help." Moving closer he put his right arm around my shoulder and led me to a chair.

"Sit down," he said, "relax."

Automatically I obeyed. He sat at the desk across from me and studied my face.

Who is he, another interrogator, I wondered?

The solitary lamp on the desk lit his face brightly. I saw good symmetrical features, a straight nose, firm mouth, dark eyebrows. Strands of blond hair partially covered his forehead. He appeared to be in his mid-twenties.

Finally, looking directly at me, he said, "poor girl, I am here to make you understand what we want from you and why. Once you see our point of view you might agree with us." The voice was kind.

"What is there to understand?" I replied. "You want me to spy on people and deliver them to you for punishment. But I can't. I won't be a murderer."

He sighed. "What a strong word, murderer. "Lara, listen. You have to hear me out. We communists are building a new society that will be the best and happiest in the history of mankind. Stalin will see to that. But we must be vigilant against our enemies. They are everywhere. Capitalists want to crush and enslave us." Taking a deep breath he went on. "Look, your friend Grisha and others participate in a subversive organization, dangerous to our cause. They and others like them must be destroyed."

A sharp, stabbing pain tore through me as he continued. "We will spread communism all over the world. Then there will be no hunger, no poverty and no war, and people will be happy."

The man's eyes were focused on something above me as if they were looking ahead into the future. I could tell that he believed what he said, and that like Olga, he had been thoroughly brainwashed.

Looking intently into my eyes, the young man added, "We need you, girl. You can be an important link in reaching our goal. How about it?"

As I listened to his appeal I knew that I could never embrace communistic ideology and sadly resigned myself to accepting my fate, as horrible as it might be. I sagged in my chair completely exhausted.

"I am so tired, so tired. I don't care what you do to me," I whispered barely moving my lips. *Was there a trace of compassion in my interrogator's eyes?*

"If you would only trust me," he said.

I shook my head. I was feeling cold, very cold. My whole body was shivering. I could not take the pressure any more.

I stared at the pistol attached to the man's belt. Desperate thoughts suddenly possessed me. I stood up.

"All right," I said. "You offered to help me, so help me." It was like I was in a trance. "I know what my punishment will be if I don't do what you want me to do. I will be sent to a concentration camp where I will die a slow painful death, or worse. You have a gun, so shoot me. Shoot me, I beg you."

The interrogator stood up. "What are you saying, girl? Shoot you? Here? Right now?"

"Don't you shoot people during interrogations?" I almost shouted. "I am an enemy of the state, you will be justified. I mean it; shoot me! When I am dead, maybe NKVD will forget about my parents."

We faced each other.

"Please," I begged, growing desperate, "do it now. Hurry."

A that moment the door opened and another official walked in. We both turned to face him. He was short and skinny with a mustache like Stalin's.

Slanted eyes regarded me with malice. I took a couple of steps back.

"Did she sign the consent?" The new NKVD man asked. I could feel evil emanating from him.

"Not yet," my young interrogator said, looking embarrassed. "I need more time. She will understand soon."

"More time for meaningless chatter?" The man exploded. "You've wasted enough time, comrade, I will deal with her myself."

I realized I was now in the hands of a pitiless interrogator who would show no mercy. I could barely stand. I staggered to my chair and slumped down. The man pushed the consent paper toward me.

"Sign it," he barked. Hypnotized by terror, I stared at his ugly face. My head was spinning.

"I don't feel well," I whispered.

"Don't feel well," he mocked. "This will teach you to feel better!" Brutally, he hit me across the face. My head jerked sideways. Pain, sharp pain.

"Comrade, don't spoil my merchandise," purred a new voice. Blearily my eyes went to the door. To my horror I recognized our former NKVD tenant who had tried to attack me last year. Slowly, he approached, fixing his gaze upon me like a reptile mesmerizing its prey. His hand touched my bruised cheek.

"You thought you escaped me, girl? Do you know it was my idea to bring you here?"

Turning to the other two men he said, "I'm claiming her for now, comrades. After I play with her a couple of days, she will cooperate beautifully, I assure you."

Grabbing my hand he pulled me off the chair. There was no resistance left in me. I felt like a zombie. No one spoke as my tormentor began to lead me out of the room. Suddenly, a tall, heavy-set man appeared at the doorway. The three NKVD men snapped to attention. An ominous silence surrounded us. The newcomer approached me. His stare was cold.

"So you are the girl," he said at last. Turning to the men he ordered, "Take her home."

"Take her home?" All three men exclaimed at once.

"She didn't sign the consent form," the short one protested.

There was a look of scorn on the big man's face. "Never mind that. I told you to take her home."

The young interrogator took a step forward. "I'll arrange for Lara to come with me."

Scarcely comprehending what was happening, I followed him down the long, empty corridor, out of the building and across the yard to a car parked by the wall. I felt hot, as if I had stepped into a sauna. My head ached unbearably. Cool fingers touched my forehead as the man seated me in the car.

"You are burning with fever," I heard him say.

I did not remember the ride home. There was a light in our window. Mother opened the door. I felt her arms, then darkness, envelop me.

33   THE RESCUE

I was unconscious as my parents carried me into the room and put me to bed. For more than a week I remained semi-comatose, burning up with fever. Delirious, I imagined that I lay in the deep water, sinking slowly to the bottom. Although I sensed that it was hard to breathe, it was more peaceful to drift in that watery depth than to waken and rise to the surface. Sometimes I could feel gentle touches and soft familiar voices. It was comforting.

Finally, I opened my eyes. It was morning and gentle sun rays were peeking through the window. I tried to get up, but my head fell back on the pillow. I felt very weak. I noticed mother sitting in the corner of the room, sewing. The needle went rhythmically back and forth. I lay quiet for a while, trying to adjust to consciousness. Suddenly the events of that horrible night came vividly back. Could it have been a nightmare? But, no. I remembered all the details of the interrogations, all three of them. And then the one, our former tenant who ... oh, my God! If not for that last commander who unexpectedly ordered to take me home... who was he?

I stirred and mumbled. "Mama." She looked at me and in two strides was at my bed.

"Lara, Lara, you are awake," she exclaimed joyfully. Her hand went to my forehead. "No, fever, no fever, oh thank God. You were so sick, my little one."

I could detect tears in her voice. Looking at her I said, trembling, "mama, it was so horrible, so horrible."

"Shh, child, shh. I don't want you to talk now."

"But do you know what happened to me that night?"

She put her hand over my lips. "We will talk later when you get stronger."

Rocking me like a child in her arms, she whispered, "You are alive, alive." It was comforting and peaceful.

"Where is papa," I asked.

"He is standing in line for milk."

"I am thirsty," I said. Soon I was drinking hot tea and mama made me a piece of buttered bread.

"Now rest," she ordered. Thankfully, I closed my eyes and drifted into a healthy and deep sleep.

I was recuperating slowly and told my parents what happened that night.

"I couldn't sign the consent to be a spy; I couldn't. It was just like consenting to be a murderer," I said, looking at them pleadingly.

"There was no other way," papa said, stroking my head.

"My poor little girl, what a monstrous and terrible system. God, what happened to good, noble Russia?"

I was getting stronger, but pain and hatred were inside me. Hatred of the Soviet Union and Stalin.

Then mama told her story. They searched for me in the village that evening and finally realized, knowing the Communist's methods, that I might be abducted, arrested. The night was terrible and at five o'clock in the morning, mama went to Tatiana Nikolajevna's house. Knowing that her husband and his brother were top ranking Communists, she asked for help to locate me.

At first, Boria's father refused to interfere.

"Look, it is too dangerous for us," he told his wife.

"I know, I know," she said. "But I worked with Lara for half a year. We are ready for concert. Where am I going to find another pianist now? And then your son, he is so attached to Lara. You want him to stop eating again?"

Her husband was shaking his head, but she persisted.

"Just call NKVD. Just call."

Finally, the man said, "All right, I will try," and left the room. It seemed ages until he came back and said, "Lara is arrested and is being interrogated at headquarters."

"My heart sank," mother remembered. "Can you help," she whispered.

"Yes," his wife added, "your brother is the head of NKVD; I am sure he can do something."

"My dear wife, I told you already how dangerous it is for me to interfere. You must understand that," he stressed.

Tatiana Nikolajevna hesitated a moment and then said, "I understand, but your brother owes you a favor. Remember, you saved his life once."

There was silence. Then the man turned around and left the room.

Mama prayed silently. Time drifted slowly. Finally, he came back and said, "Lara will be brought home shortly."

Now I understood that it was Boria's uncle who ordered my release. But now what was ahead? Will the Communists leave me be? What kind of system have they established when people who were almost children are forced to be informers, taking upon their consciences other people's lives?

Reluctantly, I started school, but kept to myself. I saw Vasia and Olga. I went to Tatiana Nikolajevna and thanked her and her husband for saving me.

"Let's not talk about it any more, Lara," she sad sadly.

We started practicing again and by the end of May gave the concert. It was a resounding success. Tatiana Nikolajevna possessed a beautiful voice. I thought, *No matter what, life goes on.*

It was an ordeal to attend school. Automatically I did my assignments. Graduation was set for the middle of June. I wished it would be sooner. I could hardly talk to my classmates.

"Lara, you've changed so much after your sickness," some would say.

There were more arrests of young people. I went to play with Boria once a week. He was such a lovely little boy. My life went on, somehow.

At the end of May as I was on my way to school from the train station, a disturbing incident occurred. On the corner of the street stood a man. He was dressed in plain clothes, but I recognized with horror that he was the young man who interrogated me that night. He looked straight at me. In front of me an elderly woman was walking. I approached her and said, "Can I walk with you? Please talk to me."

She looked at me and seeing the panic on my face said, "Of course, girl. Are you going to school?"

I nodded.

"I am going that way, too."

We passed the man. I did not look at him. My heart was in my mouth. I tried to talk to the woman about something. After a while, I turned around. The man was gone. The school was close, so I thanked my companion and ran ahead.

I could not concentrate on any subject. What did the NKVD want from me? I realized that the ordeal was not over. Too frightened to leave the school, I lingered by the door, but then remembered that there was a path to the railroad station by the river. It was longer to walk, but I had time.

I walked slowly, breathing in the fresh air. The river was flowing peacefully, surrounded by greenery. Wildflowers were everywhere. Warm sun rays were caressing my face. It was peaceful and beautiful, it felt as if for the first time in years there were no nightmares in my life.

Dear God, can you help me, please, I whispered.

I did not tell my parents about the man. They had suffered enough already. Now I always took the back road to school, watching for him carefully.

The fifteenth of June and graduation was fast approaching. I got my high school diploma. A hammer and sickle were printed on the front page, an emblem of slavery.

At least I don't have to commute to school any more, I said to myself, walking slowly by the river. It was hot and humid.

Would be nice to swim. I should have taken my bathing suit, I mused. There was a fallen stump right by the water's edge. I sat down and put my hand in the water. It felt cool and refreshing. Peaceful, peaceful. I tried to drift into that peacefulness. The horror in which I lived for almost two years seemed to melt and float away. Little fish were swimming by my hand. I made a move and they scattered away. It was funny. I laughed. It felt strange to laugh.

Suddenly, I heard a noise. I turned and to my horror saw the young man, the same young man who had been on the street corner two weeks before. I jumped up from the log, ready to run.

"Please don't run. I am here on my own. You have to hear me out," he said in one breath.

I knew I couldn't outrun him, so I just edged closer to the river bank.

"You make one step and I jump," I said, trembling.

"All I want to do is to warn you, Lara."

He remembered my name, I thought. "Warn me?"

I will be short. Remember the commissar who ordered your release," he asked.

I nodded.

"Well, this man is to be called back to Moscow by first of July. He won't be able to protect you anymore."

We stood facing each other. The information was sinking slowly into my mind. I tried to comprehend the gravity of it. The man spoke again.

"The other man, the one who... you know which one. He will be the head of NKVD." Pausing for a second, he added, almost in a whisper, "He didn't forget you."

My legs felt weak and I sat back on the log.

"My God, I will be arrested again," I mumbled under my breath.

The man took a couple of steps and sat on the log next to me. I stared ahead, without seeing anything. Then I asked, "Why are you warning me? Isn't it dangerous for you?"

"Yes, it is very dangerous. If they knew, I would be sent to a concentration camp. But something is changing in me," his face became stern. "I don't understand, myself. Before, I thought at least that I was working for the good of my country. But now, I am not sure. It hurts me to think what will happen to you."

I sat silently, my eyes following the flow of the river. Birds were flying low over the water.

"It is going to rain tomorrow," I said. The man looked at me startled.

"What I said is not scaring you?"

I shrugged my shoulders. "It is a death sentence, is it not?"

"What do you mean," he asked.

I got up. "I have a train to catch and you'd better go, too. I hope nobody has seen us, for your sake. And thanks. You don't know how thankful I am for your warning."

I looked at the man, trying to remember his face. Then I turned around and followed the path to the station.

I have only two weeks, only two weeks, I thought, *then I will be arrested again and...*

The train was almost ready to leave. I found an empty compartment; I could not face the people. It was hot and stuffy. I sat down in the corner next to the window and opened it. When the train started, the cool wind blowing into my face felt good. Words were forming by themselves in my brain.

This is it, this is it. That is the end. The arrest and...

I remembered what the NKVD man was telling me that horrible night.

I can't go through with it, I can't. I'd rather die. Yes, Lara, this is the solution, and you'd better get used to that thought. Two weeks, I have only two weeks. This refrain ran continuously through my mind.

From the train station I walked home like a mindless fly. I told my parents about the man's warning and my thoughts. For a long time there was a silence in the room. I looked quietly at their solemn faces.

"Mama, papa, I cannot go on living like this. I will die anyway in a concentration camp, but what horror will I go through before? You have to let me die."

"That is the end of us, too," mama said softly and added, "We don't want you to go through that horror."

Papa was gently stroking my head. I had a feeling that the decision was made for all of us.

The next day father went to a friend of his who was a doctor and brought a small bottle of pills and said, "This will be enough for the three of us."

Mama went to Vasia's mother and gave her all our jewelry and gold coins. "It is possible we will be deported soon, so keep these," she explained.

I went to play with Boria with a heavy heart. Tatiana Nikolajevna opened the door.

"Good," she said, letting me in. "I have to talk to you."

Looking at me significantly, she said, "We are recalled back to Moscow by the end of June and my husband's brother, too."

"I am sorry," I whispered. "It is because of me, because you helped me."

Tatiana Nikolajevna made a couple of steps towards me and embraced me. "I learned to like you very much, Lara." Her voice was cracking. "Now go and play with Boria."

My eyes filled with tears when I greeted the little boy. We played a little. He was happy to go back to Moscow.

"I have lots of friends and relations there and they like to play with me, not like the kids here."

When I was leaving, Boria asked, "Can you come and visit us in Moscow?"

I hesitated and then said, "I think that will be difficult, Boria."

A few days passed. I went for long walks in the woods. The weather was nice and warm. I was trying to inhale the beauty of nature and allow myself to part with it. Was I scared? Of course I was scared, but, there must be something on the other side. So maybe it has to be that way. Maybe I meet the other members of my family that went before me mama's mama and papa's mother and father. And mama and papa will be with me. I prayed, *Dear God, please help me to understand.*

Did I have any doubts about the decision? *Yes.* Do I have the right to take my parents' lives? But what kind of life will they have without me? I was asking myself, *Do we want to live under this murdering, jailing, exiling system; must I submit to the brutal destruction of souls and minds of communism?* But often I simply thought of myself. *You are a coward, Lara.*

Nights were hard. I couldn't sleep. I thought about the young man from NKVD who, with great danger to himself, decided to warn me. The employees of NKVD were dedicated communists, cruel and ruthless. Why did he want to work there? He explained to me that he believed in communism as a goal of a bright future. Were his beliefs beginning to crumble?

Once father explained to me that Soviet citizens are brainwashed from the start of their lives. The life is so hard that women have to work in order to supplement their husband's income. When a woman gives birth to a baby, she is allowed to stay home for only two months. Then the child is taken to special government facility until he is three years old. Soviet propaganda already starts there. At home, children sing songs praising Stalin.

From three to seven, it is preschool. The child enters the *Pioneer* organization. There, again, is communist teaching. They are taught that the Soviet Union is the best country in the world, that Stalin, "Father of the Nation," as he is called, is taking care of all the people. That in the West, people drop dead on the streets from hunger. Granted, the life is still hard now, but the future will be wonderful.

Then in high school, there is another youth organization, *Comsomol*. There young students are drilled with more communist edicts and are taught to be constantly on their guard against a counter revolution. They are encouraged to report any suspicion of anti-Soviet feelings.

The young man was raised that way. He believed in all the lies. But now, maybe... was he doubting his conviction? How could I spark that in someone so devoted? Was this hope?

34 GERMAN INVASION

It was the June twenty-first. We still had one week until July. The decision was made, but we did not talk about it and we did not set a date. It was a beautiful evening. I went outside and rested on the bench. The sun was setting. Thousands of thoughts were flying through my mind. I felt justified making the decision to end my life. But the time was getting closer and it was becoming scarier every day. To make the decision wasn't hard, but to execute it? *Oh my God,* I thought, *I am hurting so much!*

It was getting darker and darker. In a cloudless sky a few stars appeared. The moon looked calm and cold. I lingered outside, searching for peace.

"Lara, it is late. Time to go to bed." I heard mama's voice. Reluctantly, I crawled into bed and fell asleep.

Something woke me up. Some kind of noise, like thunder. Without opening my eyes, I listened. Thunder couldn't be that frequent. It sounded more like distant explosions. Explosions? I jumped out of bed. It was dawn. I noticed my father standing by the window looking out. There were dark clouds on the horizon.

"What is going on," I whispered.

Papa turned his face toward me. His eyes were shining. "I think Germans have started their offence. They are bombing the city."

Mama joined us. "I hope it's war," she said.

"War." I almost choked. "It means... it means... oh God! Then it means there is hope for us and if the Soviets are defeated, we don't need to..." I could not say the last word. Suddenly I felt weak.

Now we could distinctly hear the explosions and see dark clouds growing bigger and bigger. People started to appear on the street, looking in the same direction. We did not have a radio, so we could only assume fighting between the Germans and the Soviets had begun.

At eight o'clock in the morning, Olga burst in. "Lara!" She shouted. "The Germans have invaded us! Father had official communique. We have to pack and leave as soon as possible."

She looked at me. I tried to hide my joy, but I had a feeling she understood my thought. I said only, "I'll miss you, Olga."

"I couldn't leave you, Lara, without saying good-bye." We embraced and couldn't let go of one another. A girl from the West; a girl from the East. Throughout the whole day Soviet families were packing and leaving.

"NKVD must be leaving, too," I thought. I was in a state of euphoria. No matter what lay ahead, the axe over my head disappeared—almost. The death sentence has been dropped.

Some stores were open. There was a long line at the bakery. All three of us stood in line for more than an hour and got three loaves of bread. The next day, the Soviet Army was passing through the village. The Red Army was retreating.

It was quite late, but we couldn't sleep. We had much to talk about.

Father said, "I was fighting the Germans in the First World War. I hated them. I never thought I would be glad they are invading us."

Suddenly, there was a knock on the door. We froze. My first thought was, "NKVD has come to get me."

Another knock. Father opened the door. A Red Army soldier stood there. He looked more frightened than we.

"What do you want?" Father asked.

"I need your help," he almost whispered. "Please, I need civilian clothes."

Father understood at once—a deserter. Quietly he gathered pants, shirt, and a jacket. The soldier grabbed them and was about to turn to go, but father stopped him.

"Wait, slow down! You need shoes. You can't parade around in army boots. Luckily, we are almost the same size."

Finally, everything was tied in the bundle. Mama brought out a loaf of bread.

"God be with you," she said.

"Thank you," the man mumbled shyly, and disappeared.

"Deserters," I said, "soldiers don't want to fight for communism.

The next day there was not one Soviet family left.

Fighting was getting closer and closer to the village. Bombs were failing nearer to us. We were hiding in the cellar together with other villagers. The whole day and night the fighting went on. We sat close to each other in one corner of the cellar. I don't know why, but I was not frightened in the least.

Finally, it became quiet. For what seemed a long time, nobody wanted to move. Then we heard the shouts, "Germans are here! Germans are here!"

Slowly we walked up the stairs. The sun was piercing through the trees. It was early morning. An armored division of Germans was passing through the main road of the village. Solders walked on both sides of the road.

I stood silently, looking at them. It was hard to believe the Soviet nightmare was over. I thought, *I don't care what lies ahead, maybe another horror, but right now I don't need to die.* For the first time in almost two years, I slept soundly that night.

The next few days, we were adjusting to German rule. Curfew was established from eight o'clock in the evening until six o'clock in the morning. After a week, we decided to go back to the city, back home. We would have to walk twelve kilometers. There were rumors that half of the city was destroyed.

We started early, because the day promised to be hot. I walked joyfully, filled with hope. *I will see Vasia and his mother, my friends and neighbors,* I rambled. It was just a miracle. I had to adjust to the thought that I didn't have to die and felt overcome with life.

There was a horrible stench when we were passing through the woods. Nobody was burying the fallen soldiers. On the open road we encountered broken tanks, trucks, airplanes, and other army equipment.

Walking through the city we noticed how much damage it had sustained. My heart pounded. Just around the corner should be our house. Maybe it burned too? But it stood, some of it. It had been half destroyed by a bomb. But the house where Vasia and his mother used to live had been burned to the ground.

The neighbors started to gather, greeting us. Vasia came running with his mother. It was such a joyous reunion. We all cried. I was overjoyed, *I am home! I am home!*

Neighbors brought some things so we could stay overnight. Two rooms and the kitchen were livable. Vasia's mother invited us to share their meal. Everybody was glad to see us.

In late afternoon, my friend Lida dropped in. We held each other in a long embrace. She told me about our school friends; some of them had been killed. Then she said, "You know, Grisha is alive."

"Grisha's alive?" I shouted, "He was imprisoned."

"Yes, he was in prison, but before the communists evacuated, they brought all the prisoners out to the courtyard and shot them with machine guns and left them there. Grisha was wounded, but not seriously. He just lost lots of blood. He hid underneath some dead bodies for two days. Then the Germans found him and took him to their field hospital."

"How about his aunt?" I asked.

"Neighbors found her sitting in a chair, dead, two days before the war."

"My God. How awful. Poor Grisha, how will he take it?"

It was too much sorrow and happiness mixed into the moment. I wasn't sure just how to feel.

Finally, we settled down. I tried to fall asleep, but couldn't, so I went out on the balcony. It was a clear, warm night. Stars twinkled. The moon shone above the castle.

Like two years ago, I reminisced. *So much has happened in those two years. I lived through the nightmare. I am not the same happy girl thinking of a bright future... but no matter, I am alive and ready to do some more living.*

I felt sadness like a wound in my chest. But, the feeling of being alive and free of Stalin was worth it. I knew I could face the world again tomorrow.

The End

Printed in the United States
58599LVS00001B/1-81